100 Best Appetizer Recipes

Publications International, Ltd.
Favorite Brand Name Recipes at www.fbnr.com

Microwave Cooking: Microwave ovens vary in wattage. Use the cooking times as guidelines and check for doneness before adding more time.

Preparation/Cooking Times: Preparation times are based on the approximate amount of time required to assemble the recipe before cooking, baking, chilling or serving. These times include preparation steps such as measuring, chopping and mixing. The fact that some preparations and cooking can be done simultaneously is taken into account. Preparation of optional ingredients and serving suggestions is not included.

TABLE OF CONTENTS

Pizza Fondue, page 50

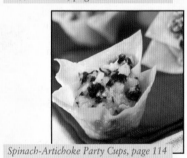

Spinach-Artichoke Party Cups, page 114

Nicole's Cheddar Crisps, page 198

FAMOUS CLASSICS

Original Ranch® Snack Mix

8 cups KELLOGG'S® CRISPIX® cereal
2½ cups small pretzels
2½ cups bite-size Cheddar cheese crackers (optional)
3 tablespoons vegetable oil
1 packet (1 ounce) HIDDEN VALLEY® The Original Ranch®
Salad Dressing & Seasoning Mix

Combine cereal, pretzels and crackers in a gallon-size Glad® Zipper Storage Bag. Pour oil over mixture. Seal bag and toss to coat. Add salad dressing & seasoning mix; seal bag and toss again until coated.

Makes 10 cups

Original Ranch® Oyster Crackers

1 box (16 ounces) oyster crackers
¼ cup vegetable oil
1 packet (1 ounce) HIDDEN VALLEY® The Original Ranch®
Salad Dressing & Seasoning Mix

Place crackers in a gallon size Glad® Fresh Protection Bag. Pour oil over crackers and toss to coat. Add salad dressing mix; toss again until coated. Bake at 250°F for 15 to 20 minutes.

Makes 8 cups

Top to bottom: Original Ranch® Snack Mix
and Original Ranch® Oyster Crackers

Hot Artichoke Dip

1 envelope LIPTON® RECIPE SECRETS® Onion Soup Mix*
1 can (14 ounces) artichoke hearts, drained and chopped
1 cup HELLMANN'S® or BEST FOODS® Mayonnaise
1 container (8 ounces) sour cream
1 cup shredded Swiss or mozzarella cheese (about 4 ounces)

*Also terrific with LIPTON® RECIPE SECRETS® Savory Herb with Garlic, Golden Onion or Onion-Mushroom Soup Mix.

1. Preheat oven to 350°F. In 1-quart casserole, combine all ingredients.

2. Bake, uncovered, 30 minutes or until heated through.

3. Serve with your favorite dippers.   *Makes 3 cups dip*

Cold Artichoke Dip: Omit Swiss cheese. Stir in, if desired, ¼ cup grated Parmesan cheese. Do not bake.

Serving Suggestion: When serving hot dip for a party, try baking it in 2 smaller casseroles. When the first casserole is empty, replace it with the second one, fresh from the oven.

Zesty Liver Pâté

⅓ cup butter or margarine
1 pound chicken livers
¾ cup coarsely chopped green onions
¾ cup chopped fresh parsley
½ cup dry white wine
¾ teaspoon TABASCO® brand Pepper Sauce
½ teaspoon salt
   Crackers or French bread

Melt butter in large saucepan; add chicken livers, onions and parsley. Sauté until livers are evenly browned and cooked through. Transfer to blender or food processor container. Add wine, TABASCO® Sauce and salt; cover. Process until smooth. Pour into decorative crock-style jar with lid. Chill until thick enough to spread. Serve with crackers or French bread.

Makes about 2 cups pâté

FAMOUS CLASSICS

Hot Artichoke Dip

Spicy Shrimp Cocktail

2 tablespoons olive or vegetable oil
¼ cup finely chopped onion
1 tablespoon chopped green bell pepper
1 clove garlic, minced
1 can (8 ounces) CONTADINA® Tomato Sauce
1 tablespoon chopped pitted green olives, drained
¼ teaspoon red pepper flakes
1 pound cooked shrimp, chilled

1. Heat oil in small skillet. Add onion, bell pepper and garlic; sauté until vegetables are tender. Stir in tomato sauce, olives and red pepper flakes.

2. Bring to a boil; simmer, uncovered, for 5 minutes. Cover.

3. Chill thoroughly. Combine sauce with shrimp in small bowl.

Makes 8 servings

Prep Time: 6 minutes
Cook Time: 10 minutes

Ortega® 7-Layer Dip

1 can (16 ounces) ORTEGA® Refried Beans
1 package (1.25 ounces) ORTEGA® Taco Seasoning Mix
1 container (8 ounces) sour cream
1 container (8 ounces) refrigerated guacamole
1 cup (4 ounces) shredded Cheddar cheese
1 cup ORTEGA® Salsa Prima Homestyle Mild or Thick & Chunky
1 can (4 ounces) ORTEGA® Diced Green Chiles
2 large green onions, sliced
Tortilla chips

COMBINE beans and seasoning mix in small bowl. Spread bean mixture in 8-inch square baking dish.

TOP with sour cream, guacamole, cheese, salsa, chiles and green onions. Serve with chips.

Makes 10 to 12 servings

Note: Can be prepared up to 2 hours ahead and refrigerated.

Spicy Shrimp Cocktail

Artichoke Frittata

1 can (14 ounces) artichoke hearts, drained
1 tablespoon olive oil, divided
½ cup minced green onions
5 eggs
½ cup (2 ounces) shredded Swiss cheese
2 tablespoons grated Parmesan cheese
1 tablespoon minced fresh parsley
1 teaspoon salt
   Freshly ground black pepper to taste

1. Chop artichoke hearts; set aside.

2. Heat 2 teaspoons oil in 10-inch skillet over medium heat. Add green onions; cook and stir until tender. Remove from skillet.

3. Beat eggs in medium bowl until light. Stir in artichokes, green onions, cheeses, parsley, salt and pepper.

4. Heat remaining 1 teaspoon oil in same skillet over medium heat. Pour egg mixture into skillet. Cook 4 to 5 minutes or until bottom is lightly browned. Place large plate over skillet and invert frittata onto plate. Return frittata, uncooked side down, to skillet. Cook about 4 minutes more or until center is just set. Cut into small wedges.   *Makes 12 to 16 appetizer servings*

Lipton® Onion Dip

1 envelope LIPTON® RECIPE SECRETS® Onion Soup Mix
1 container (16 ounces) sour cream

1. In medium bowl, combine ingredients; chill, if desired.

2. Serve with your favorite dippers.   *Makes 2 cups dip*

Salsa Onion Dip: Stir in ½ cup of your favorite salsa.

Prep Time: 5 minutes

Artichoke Frittata

Gorgonzola Buffalo Wings

DRESSING

- ¼ **cup mayonnaise**
- 3 **tablespoons sour cream**
- 1½ **tablespoons white wine vinegar**
- ¼ **teaspoon sugar**
- ⅓ **cup (1½ ounces) BELGIOIOSO® Gorgonzola**

CHICKEN

- 2 **pounds chicken wings**
- 3 **tablespoons hot pepper sauce**
- 1 **tablespoon vegetable oil**
- 1 **clove garlic, minced**

FOR DRESSING

Combine mayonnaise, sour cream, vinegar and sugar in small bowl. Stir in BelGioioso Gorgonzola; cover and refrigerate until serving.

FOR CHICKEN

Place chicken in large resealable plastic food storage bag. Combine pepper sauce, oil and garlic in separate small bowl; pour over chicken. Seal bag tightly; turn to coat. Marinate in refrigerator at least 1 hour or, for hotter flavor, up to 24 hours, turning occasionally.

Prepare grill. Drain chicken, discarding marinade. Place chicken on grill. Grill on covered grill over medium-hot coals 25 to 30 minutes or until chicken is no longer pink, turning 3 to 4 times. Serve with dressing.   *Makes 8 servings*

Sweet and Sour Meatballs

MEATBALLS
- ½ **cup instant rice**
- 2 **pounds 90% lean ground beef**
- 1 **egg**
- 1 **cup soft butter-flavored cracker crumbs***
- 2 **tablespoons oil**

SAUCE
- 1½ **cups barbecue sauce**
- 1 **cup (12-ounce jar) SMUCKER'S® Pineapple Topping**
- ¼ **cup firmly packed brown sugar**

You can substitute croutons or stuffing mix for the crackers.

Prepare rice according to package directions.

Meanwhile, combine ground beef, egg and cracker crumbs; mix well. Add cooked rice; mix thoroughly. Shape into 1-inch meatballs. Cook in oil over medium heat until browned, turning occasionally. If necessary, drain grease from skillet.

Combine all sauce ingredients; mix until brown sugar is dissolved. Pour over meatballs. Cover and simmer over low heat for 30 to 45 minutes or until meatballs are no longer pink in center. Serve with toothpicks.

Makes 8 to 12 servings

TIP **To quickly shape uniform meatballs, place meat mixture on a plastic cutting board and pat evenly into a large square 1-inch thick. With a sharp knife, cut meat into 1-inch squares. Shape each square into a ball.**

Spinach Dip

**1 package (10 ounces) frozen chopped spinach, thawed and
   squeezed dry**
1 container (16 ounces) sour cream
1 cup HELLMANN'S® or BEST FOODS® Mayonnaise
**1 package KNORR® Recipe Classics™ Vegetable Soup, Dip and
   Recipe Mix**
**1 can (8 ounces) water chestnuts, drained and chopped
   (optional)**
3 green onions, chopped

- In medium bowl, combine all ingredients; chill at least 2 hours to blend flavors.

- Stir before serving. Serve with your favorite dippers.

Makes about 4 cups dip

Yogurt Spinach Dip: Substitute 1 container (16 ounces) plain lowfat yogurt for sour cream.

Spinach and Cheese Dip: Add 2 cups (8 ounces) shredded Swiss cheese with spinach.

Prep Time: 10 minutes
Chill Time: 2 hours

Spicy Cheese 'n' Chili Dip

1 pound BOB EVANS® Special Seasonings Roll Sausage
1 pound pasteurized process cheese spread
1 (10-ounce) can diced tomatoes with green chiles, drained
1 (14- to 16-ounce) bag tortilla chips

Crumble and cook sausage in medium skillet until browned. Drain on paper towels. Combine cheese and tomatoes in medium saucepan; heat until cheese is melted. Stir in sausage. Serve in warm bowl with tortilla chips.

Makes 10 to 12 servings

Spinach Dip

The Ultimate Onion

3 cups cornstarch
3½ cups all-purpose flour, divided
6 teaspoons paprika, divided
2 teaspoons garlic salt
1 teaspoon salt
1½ teaspoons black pepper, divided
2 bottles (24 ounces) beer
4 to 6 Colossal onions (4 inches in diameter)
2 teaspoons garlic powder
¾ teaspoon cayenne pepper, divided
1 pint mayonnaise (2 cups)
1 pint sour cream (2 cups)
½ cup chili sauce

1. For batter, mix cornstarch, 1½ cups flour, 2 teaspoons paprika, garlic salt, salt and 1 teaspoon black pepper in large bowl. Add beer; mix well. Set aside.

2. Cut about ¾-inch off top of each onion; peel onions. Being careful not to cut through bottom, cut onions into 12 to 16 wedges.

3. Soak cut onions in ice water for 10 to 15 minutes. If onions do not "bloom," cut petals slightly deeper. Meanwhile, prepare seasoned flour mixture. Combine remaining 2 cups flour, remaining 4 teaspoons paprika, garlic powder, remaining ½ teaspoon black pepper and ¼ teaspoon cayenne pepper in large bowl; mix well.

4. Dip cut onions into seasoned flour; remove excess by carefully shaking. Dip in batter; remove excess by carefully shaking. Separate "petals" to coat thoroughly with batter. (If batter begins to separate, mix thoroughly before using.)

5. Gently place onions, one at a time, in fryer basket and deep-fry at 375°F 1½ minutes. Turn onion over and fry 1 to 1½ minutes or until golden brown. Drain on paper towels. Place onion upright in shallow bowl and remove about 1 inch of "petals" from center of onion.

6. To prepare Creamy Chili Sauce, combine mayonnaise, sour cream, chili sauce and remaining ½ teaspoon cayenne pepper in large bowl; mix well. Serve warm onions with Creamy Chili Sauce.   *Makes about 24 servings*

*Favorite recipe from **National Onion Association***

The Ultimate Onion

Nutty Bacon Cheeseball

1 package (8 ounces) cream cheese, softened
½ cup milk
2 cups (8 ounces) shredded sharp Cheddar cheese
2 cups (8 ounces) shredded Monterey Jack cheese
¼ cup (1 ounce) crumbled blue cheese
¼ cup finely minced green onions (white parts only)
1 jar (2 ounces) diced pimiento, drained
10 slices bacon, cooked, drained, finely crumbled and divided
¾ cup finely chopped pecans, divided
Salt and black pepper to taste
¼ cup minced parsley
1 tablespoon poppy seeds

Beat cream cheese and milk on low speed in large bowl with electric mixer until blended. Add cheeses. Blend on medium speed until well combined. Add green onions, pimiento, half of bacon and half of pecans. Blend on medium speed until well mixed. Add salt and pepper to taste. Transfer half of mixture to large piece of plastic wrap. Form into ball; wrap tightly. Repeat with remaining mixture. Refrigerate until chilled, at least two hours.

Combine remaining bacon and pecans with parsley and poppy seeds in pie plate or large dinner plate. Remove plastic wrap from each ball; roll each in bacon mixture until well coated. Wrap each ball tightly in plastic wrap and refrigerate until ready to use, up to 24 hours.   *Makes about 24 servings*

TIP To soften cream cheese quickly, remove cheese from the wrapper and place in a medium microwave-safe bowl. Microwave at MEDIUM (50% power) 15 to 20 seconds or until slightly softened.

Nutty Bacon Cheeseball

Cheese Straws

½ cup (1 stick) butter, softened
⅛ teaspoon salt
Dash ground red pepper
1 pound sharp Cheddar cheese, shredded, at room temperature
2 cups self-rising flour

Heat oven to 350°F. In mixer bowl, beat butter, salt and pepper until creamy. Add cheese; mix well. Gradually add flour, mixing until dough begins to form a ball. Form dough into ball with hands. Fit cookie press with small star plate; fill with dough according to manufacturer's directions. Press dough onto cookie sheets in 3-inch-long strips (or desired shapes). Bake 12 minutes, just until lightly browned. Cool completely on wire rack. Store tightly covered.

Makes about 10 dozen

*Favorite recipe from **Southeast United Dairy Industry Association, Inc.***

Potato Skins

4 baked potatoes, quartered
¼ cup sour cream
1 packet (1 ounce) HIDDEN VALLEY® The Original Ranch® Salad Dressing & Seasoning Mix
1 cup (4 ounces) shredded Cheddar cheese
Sliced green onions and/or bacon pieces* (optional)

*Crisp-cooked, crumbled bacon can be used.

Scoop potato out of skins; combine potatoes with sour cream and salad dressing & seasoning mix. Fill skins with mixture. Sprinkle with cheese. Bake at 375°F. for 12 to 15 minutes or until cheese is melted. Garnish with green onions and/or bacon bits, if desired.

Makes 8 to 10 servings

Cheese Straws

7-Layer Ranch Dip

1 envelope LIPTON® RECIPE SECRETS® Ranch Soup Mix
1 container (16 ounces) sour cream
1 cup shredded lettuce
1 medium tomato, chopped (about 1 cup)
1 can (2.25 ounces) sliced pitted ripe olives, drained
¼ cup chopped red onion
1 can (4.5 ounces) chopped green chilies, drained
1 cup shredded Cheddar cheese (about 4 ounces)

1. In 2-quart shallow dish, combine soup mix and sour cream.

2. Evenly layer remaining ingredients, ending with cheese. Chill, if desired.
Serve with tortilla chips.   *Makes 7 cups dip*

Prep Time: 15 minutes

Awesome Antipasto

1 jar (16 ounces) mild cherry peppers, drained
1 jar (9 ounces) artichoke hearts, drained
½ pound asparagus spears, cooked
½ cup pitted black olives
1 red onion, cut into thin wedges
1 green bell pepper, sliced into rings
1 red bell pepper, sliced into rings
1 bottle (8 ounces) Italian salad dressing
1 cup shredded Parmesan cheese, divided
1 package (6 ounces) HILLSHIRE FARM® Hard Salami

Layer cherry peppers, artichoke hearts, asparagus, olives, onion and bell
peppers in 13×9-inch glass baking dish.

Pour dressing and ⅓ cup cheese over vegetables. Cover; refrigerate 1 to
2 hours.

Drain vegetables, reserving marinade. Arrange vegetables and Hard Salami in
rows on serving platter. Drizzle with reserved marinade. Top with remaining
⅔ cup cheese.   *Makes 6 to 8 servings*

7-Layer Ranch Dip

Festive Franks

1 can (8 ounces) reduced-fat crescent roll dough
5½ teaspoons barbecue sauce
⅓ cup finely shredded reduced-fat sharp Cheddar cheese
8 fat-free hot dogs
¼ teaspoon poppy seeds (optional)
Additional barbecue sauce (optional)

1. Preheat oven to 350°F. Spray large baking sheet with nonstick cooking spray; set aside.

2. Unroll dough and separate into 8 triangles. Cut each triangle in half lengthwise to make 2 triangles. Lightly spread barbecue sauce over each triangle. Sprinkle with cheese.

3. Cut each hot dog in half; trim off rounded ends. Place one hot dog piece at large end of one dough triangle. Roll up jelly-roll style from wide end. Place point-side down on prepared baking sheet. Sprinkle with poppy seeds, if desired. Repeat with remaining hot dog pieces and dough.

4. Bake 13 minutes or until dough is golden brown. Cool 1 to 2 minutes on baking sheet. Serve with additional barbecue sauce for dipping, if desired.

Makes 16 servings

Buffalo-Style Chicken Nachos

2 cups diced cooked chicken
⅓ cup *Frank's® RedHot®* Cayenne Pepper Sauce
2 tablespoons melted butter
1 bag (10 ounces) tortilla chips
3 cups shredded Cheddar or Monterey Jack cheese

1. Preheat oven to 350°F. Combine chicken, *Frank's RedHot* Sauce and butter. Layer chips, chicken and cheese in ovenproof serving dish or baking dish.

2. Bake 5 minutes just until cheese melts. Garnish as desired. Splash on more *Frank's RedHot* Sauce to taste.

Makes 4 to 8 servings

Prep Time: 5 minutes
Cook Time: 5 minutes

Festive Franks

FAST & FABULOUS

Creamy Garlic Salsa Dip

**1 envelope LIPTON® RECIPE SECRETS® Savory Herb with
  Garlic Soup Mix***
1 container (16 ounces) sour cream
½ cup your favorite prepared salsa

*Also terrific with LIPTON® RECIPE SECRETS® Onion Soup Mix.

1. In medium bowl, combine all ingredients; chill at least 2 hours.

2. Serve with your favorite dippers.   *Makes 2½ cups dip*

Alouette® Elégante
with Red Pepper Coulis

1 small jar roasted red peppers, drained
1 teaspoon olive oil
**1 (6-ounce) package ALOUETTE® Elégante, Roasted Garlic
  and Pesto**
Paprika
Fresh chopped chives or parsley

To make red pepper coulis, add roasted red peppers and olive oil to food
processor; purée until smooth. Pour coulis into center of 8-inch rimmed
salad plate (a plain white plate works best). Position Alouette Elégante in
center of coulis. Sprinkle paprika and chopped chives around rim of plate.
Serve with your favorite crusty bread.   *Makes 6 to 8 servings*

Creamy Garlic Salsa Dip

Piggy Wraps

1 package HILLSHIRE FARM® Lit'l Smokies
2 cans (8 ounces each) refrigerated crescent roll dough,
cut into small triangles

Preheat oven to 400°F.

Wrap individual Lit'l Smokies in dough triangles. Bake 5 minutes or until golden brown. *Makes about 50 hors d'oeuvres*

Note: Piggy Wraps may be frozen. To reheat in microwave, microwave at HIGH (100% power) 1½ minutes or at MEDIUM-HIGH (70% power) 2 minutes. When reheated in microwave, dough will not be crisp.

Smoked Turkey Roll-Ups

2 packages (4 ounces each) herb-flavored soft spreadable cheese
4 flour (8-inch diameter) tortillas*
2 packages (6 ounces each) smoked turkey breast slices
2 green onions, minced
¼ cup roasted red peppers, drained and finely chopped

*To keep flour tortillas soft while preparing turkey roll-ups, cover with a slightly damp cloth.

1. Spread one package of cheese evenly over tortillas. Layer turkey slices evenly and over cheese, overlapping turkey slices slightly to cover each tortilla. Spread remaining package of cheese evenly over turkey slices. Sprinkle with green onions and red peppers.

2. Roll up each tortilla jelly-roll style. Place roll-ups, seam side down, in resealable plastic bag; refrigerate several hours or overnight.

3. To serve, cut each roll-up crosswise into ½-inch slices to form pinwheels. If desired, arrange pinwheels on serving plate and garnish with red pepper slices in center. *Makes 56 appetizer servings*

*Favorite recipe from **National Turkey Federation***

Top to bottom: Piggy Wraps and Lit'l Party
Delights (page 110)

Pizza Snack Cups

1 can (12 ounces) refrigerated biscuits (10 biscuits)
½ pound ground beef
1 jar (14 ounces) RAGÚ® Pizza Quick® Sauce
½ cup shredded mozzarella cheese (about 2 ounces)

1. Preheat oven to 375°F. In muffin pan, evenly press each biscuit in bottom and up side of cups; chill until ready to fill.

2. In 10-inch skillet, brown ground beef over medium-high heat; drain. Stir in Ragú Pizza Quick Sauce and heat through.

3. Evenly spoon beef mixture into prepared muffin cups. Bake 15 minutes. Sprinkle with cheese and bake an additional 5 minutes or until cheese is melted and biscuits are golden. Let stand 5 minutes. Gently remove pizza cups from muffin pan and serve.   *Makes 10 pizza cups*

Prep Time: 10 minutes
Cook Time: 25 minutes

Brandied Apricot Brie

1 wheel ALOUETTE® Baby Brie™, Plain
1 cup apricot preserves
1 tablespoon freshly squeezed orange juice
2 teaspoons brandy
1 teaspoon ground cinnamon
1 loaf French bread, sliced

MICROWAVE DIRECTIONS

Combine preserves, orange juice, brandy and cinnamon in microwave-safe bowl. Cover with plastic wrap and microwave on HIGH (100% power) 1½ minutes or until sauce begins to bubble. Place ALOUETTE® Baby Brie™ in shallow dish and top with apricot sauce. Microwave, uncovered, on HIGH 30 to 90 seconds or until cheese softens. Serve with French bread.

Makes 6 to 8 servings

Pizza Snack Cups

Lipton® Ranch Dip

1 envelope LIPTON® RECIPE SECRETS® Ranch Soup Mix
1 container (16 ounces) sour cream

1. In medium bowl, combine ingredients; chill, if desired.

2. Serve with your favorite dippers.   *Makes 2 cups dip*

Ranch Salsa Dip: Stir in ½ cup of your favorite salsa.

Ranch Artichoke Dip: Stir in 1 jar (14 ounces) marinated artichoke hearts, drained and chopped.

Prep Time: 5 minutes

Cocktail Bites

1¼ cups red currant jelly or cranberry sauce
1¼ cups ketchup
2 pounds HILLSHIRE FARM® Lit'l Smokies

Heat jelly and ketchup in small saucepan over medium heat *or* microwave, uncovered, at HIGH 1 to 2 minutes or until mixture blends smoothly. Add Lit'l Smokies; cook until links are hot. Serve with frilled toothpicks.

Makes about 100 hors d'oeuvres

Holiday Meatballs

1 package Original or Italian Style Meatballs
1 cup HEINZ® Chili Sauce
1 cup grape jelly

Heat meatballs according to package directions. Meanwhile, in small saucepan, combine chili sauce and grape jelly. Heat until jelly is melted. Place meatballs in serving dish. Pour chili sauce mixture over meatballs; stir gently to coat. Serve warm.   *Makes 60 appetizers*

Variation: For a zestier sauce, substitute hot jalapeño jelly for grape jelly.

Top to bottom: Lipton® Onion Dip (page 10) and Lipton® Ranch Dip

Pizza Rollers

1 package (10 ounces) refrigerated pizza dough
½ cup pizza sauce
18 slices turkey pepperoni
6 sticks mozzarella cheese

1. Preheat oven to 425°F. Coat baking sheet with nonstick cooking spray.

2. Roll out pizza dough on baking sheet to form 12×9-inch rectangle. Cut pizza dough into 6 (4½×4-inch) rectangles. Spread about 1 tablespoon sauce over center third of each rectangle. Top with 3 slices pepperoni and stick of mozzarella cheese. Bring ends of dough together over cheese, pinching to seal. Place seam side down on prepared baking sheet.

3. Bake in center of oven 10 minutes or until golden brown.

Makes 6 servings

Chicken Nachos

22 (about 1 ounce) GUILTLESS GOURMET® Baked Tortilla Chips (yellow, red or blue corn)
½ cup (4 ounces) cooked and shredded boneless chicken breast
¼ cup chopped green onions
¼ cup (1 ounce) grated Cheddar cheese
Sliced green and red chilies (optional)

MICROWAVE DIRECTIONS

Spread tortilla chips on flat microwave-safe plate. Sprinkle chicken, onions and cheese over chips. Microwave on HIGH 30 seconds until cheese starts to bubble. Serve hot. Garnish with chilies, if desired.

CONVENTIONAL DIRECTIONS

Preheat oven to 325°F. Spread tortilla chips on baking sheet. Sprinkle chicken, onions and cheese over chips. Bake about 5 minutes or until cheese starts to bubble. Serve hot.

Makes 22 nachos

Pizza Rollers

Herb Cheese Twists

2 tablespoons butter or margarine
¼ cup grated Parmesan cheese
1 teaspoon dried parsley flakes
1 teaspoon dried basil leaves
1 can (7½ ounces) refrigerated buttermilk biscuits

1. Preheat oven to 400°F. Microwave butter in small bowl at MEDIUM (50% power) just until melted; cool slightly. Stir in cheese, parsley and basil. Set aside.

2. Pat each biscuit into 5×2-inch rectangle. Spread 1 teaspoon butter mixture on each rectangle; cut each in half lengthwise. Twist each strip 3 or 4 times. Place on lightly greased baking sheet. Bake 8 to 10 minutes or until golden brown. *Makes 5 servings*

Prep and Cook Time: 20 minutes

Tortilla Roll-Ups

1 (8-ounce) package cream cheese
1 cup chopped black olives
4 green onions, chopped
2 teaspoons TABASCO® brand Pepper Sauce
4 to 6 large flour tortillas

Combine cream cheese, olives, green onions and TABASCO® Sauce in medium bowl. Spread thin layer of cream cheese mixture on each tortilla. Starting at one end, gently roll tortilla into tight tube. Wrap with plastic wrap; chill until ready to serve. To serve, unwrap roll, trim edges of tortilla and slice into 8 (1-inch) slices. Serve slices cut sides up. *Makes 32 to 48 pieces*

Herb Cheese Twists

Microwave Sweet Potato Chips

2 cups thinly sliced sweet potatoes
1 tablespoon packed brown sugar
2 teaspoons margarine

Place sweet potatoes, in single layer, in microwavable dish. Sprinkle with water. Microwave at HIGH 5 minutes. Stir in brown sugar and margarine. Microwave at HIGH 2 to 3 minutes. Let stand a few minutes before serving.

Makes 4 to 6 servings

*Favorite recipe from **The Sugar Association, Inc.***

Marinated Mushrooms

2 pounds mushrooms
1 bottle (8 ounces) Italian salad dressing
Grated peel of ½ SUNKIST® lemon
Juice of 1 SUNKIST® lemon
2 tablespoons sliced pimiento (optional)
2 tablespoons chopped parsley

In large saucepan, combine mushrooms and Italian dressing; bring to a boil. Cook, uncovered, 2 to 3 minutes, stirring constantly. Add lemon peel, juice and pimiento. Chill 4 hours or more. Drain; reserve dressing. Stir in parsley. Serve as an appetizer with toothpicks. Garnish with lemon cartwheel slices, if desired.

Makes about 4 cups

Serving Suggestion: Reserved dressing may be used on salads. Makes about 1½ cups.

Variation: Substitute 1 bottle (8 ounces) reduced-calorie Italian dressing for regular Italian dressing.

Quick Pimiento Cheese Snacks

Golden Chicken Nuggets

1 pound boneless skinless chicken, cut into 1½-inch pieces
¼ cup *French's*® Sweet & Tangy Honey Mustard
2 cups *French's*® French Fried Onions, finely crushed

1. Preheat oven to 400°F. Toss chicken with mustard in medium bowl.

2. Place French Fried Onions into resealable plastic food storage bag. Toss chicken in onions, a few pieces at a time, pressing gently to adhere.

3. Place nuggets in shallow baking pan. Bake 15 minutes or until chicken is no longer pink in center. Serve with additional honey mustard.

Makes 4 to 8 servings

Prep Time: 5 minutes
Cook Time: 15 minutes

Roasted Red Pepper Dip

1 envelope LIPTON® RECIPE SECRETS® Onion Soup Mix
1 container (16 ounces) regular sour cream
1 jar (7 ounces) roasted red peppers, drained and chopped

In large bowl, blend all ingredients; chill at least 2 hours. Serve, if desired, with bread sticks, celery or carrot sticks, cooked tortellini or mozzarella sticks.

Makes 2 cups dip

Salsa Onion Dip

1 envelope LIPTON® RECIPE SECRETS® Onion Soup Mix
1 container (16 ounces) sour cream
½ cup salsa

1. In medium bowl, combine ingredients; chill, if desired.

2. Serve with your favorite dippers.

Makes 2½ cups dip

Prep Time: 5 minutes

Golden Chicken Nuggets

Summer Sausage Dippers

5 ounces sharp Cheddar cheese, cut into 1×½-inch chunks
32 pimiento-stuffed green olives
1 (9-ounce) HILLSHIRE FARM® Summer Sausage, cut into
    32 thick half-moon slices
1 cup ketchup
½ cup apricot jam or preserves
1 tablespoon cider vinegar
2 teaspoons Worcestershire sauce

Secure 1 piece cheese and 1 olive onto 1 Summer Sausage slice with frilled toothpick; repeat with remaining cheese, olives and sausage. Arrange on platter. Cover and refrigerate until ready to serve. For dipping sauce, stir ketchup, jam, vinegar and Worcestershire sauce in small saucepan; heat over medium-low heat until warm and smooth. Serve sausage dippers with sauce.

Makes 16 servings

Spicy Mustard Kielbasa Bites

1 pound whole kielbasa or smoked Polish sausage
1 cup *French's®* Bold n' Spicy Brown Mustard
¾ cup honey
1 tablespoon *Frank's® RedHot®* Cayenne Pepper Sauce

1. Place kielbasa on grid. Grill over medium heat 10 minutes or until lightly browned, turning occasionally. Cut into bite-sized pieces; set aside.

2. Combine mustard and honey in large saucepan. Bring to a boil over medium heat. Stir in kielbasa and *Frank's RedHot* Sauce. Cook until heated through. Transfer to serving bowl. Serve with party toothpicks.

Makes 16 servings

Note: Refrigerate leftover honey-mustard mixture. This makes a tasty dip for chicken nuggets, cooked chicken wings or mini hot dogs.

Prep Time: 15 minutes
Cook Time: 10 minutes

Summer Sausage Dippers

Vegetable Cream Cheese

1 envelope LIPTON® RECIPE SECRETS® Vegetable Soup Mix
2 packages (8 ounces each) cream cheese, softened
2 tablespoons milk

1. In medium bowl, combine ingredients; chill 2 hours.

2. Serve on bagels or with assorted fresh vegetables.

Makes 2½ cups spread

Prep Time: 10 minutes
Chill Time: 2 hours

Saucy Mini Franks

½ cup *French's® Sweet & Tangy Honey Mustard*
½ cup chili sauce or ketchup
½ cup grape jelly
1 tablespoon *Frank's® RedHot® Cayenne Pepper Sauce*
1 pound mini cocktail franks or 1 pound cooked meatballs

1. Combine mustard, chili sauce, grape jelly and *Frank's RedHot* Sauce in saucepan.

2. Add cocktail franks. Simmer and stir 5 minutes or until jelly is melted and franks are hot.

Makes about 12 servings

Prep Time: 5 minutes
Cook Time: 5 minutes

Ranch Chicken Tenders

2 tablespoons margarine or butter, melted
1 envelope LIPTON® RECIPE SECRETS® Ranch Soup Mix
1½ pounds chicken tenders or boneless, skinless chicken
   breast halves, cut in strips

1. In small bowl, combine margarine with soup mix. Add chicken to soup mixture and let stand 5 minutes.

2. Heat 10-inch nonstick skillet over medium-high heat 3 minutes or until hot.

3. Add chicken mixture and cook, stirring occasionally, 6 minutes or until chicken is thoroughly cooked. Serve with your favorite dipping sauce.

Makes 12 servings

Prep Time: 5 minutes
Cook Time: 6 minutes

Roasted Almonds

2 tablespoons CRISCO® Canola Oil, divided
1 pound whole blanched almonds
2 teaspoons ground cinnamon
   Confectioners' sugar

1. Heat 1 tablespoon oil in large skillet over medium heat until hot. Add ½ pound almonds. Cook and stir until evenly browned. Sprinkle with 1 teaspoon cinnamon; stir well. Place on paper towels to drain. Dust with confectioners' sugar to taste.

2. Repeat with remaining ingredients.

Makes 1 pound nuts

DIPS & SPREADS

Pizza Fondue

½ **pound bulk Italian sausage**
1 **cup chopped onion**
2 **jars (26 ounces each) meatless pasta sauce**
4 **ounces thinly sliced ham, finely chopped**
1 **package (3 ounces) sliced pepperoni, finely chopped**
¼ **teaspoon red pepper flakes**
1 **pound mozzarella cheese, cut into ¾-inch cubes**
1 **loaf Italian or French bread, cut into 1-inch cubes**

SLOW COOKER DIRECTIONS

1. Cook sausage and onion in large skillet until sausage is browned. Drain off fat.

2. Transfer sausage mixture to slow cooker. Stir in pasta sauce, ham, pepperoni and pepper flakes. Cover; cook on LOW 3 to 4 hours.

3. Serve sauce with cheese cubes, bread cubes and fondue forks.

Makes 20 to 25 appetizer servings

Prep Time: 15 minutes
Cook Time: 3 to 4 hours

Pizza Fondue

Creamy Artichoke-Parmesan Dip

2 cans (14 ounces each) quartered artichokes,
    drained and chopped
2 cups (8 ounces) shredded mozzarella cheese
1½ cups grated Parmesan cheese
1½ cups mayonnaise
  ½ cup finely chopped onion
  ½ teaspoon dried oregano leaves
  ¼ teaspoon garlic powder
    Pita wedges
    Assorted cut-up vegetables

SLOW COOKER DIRECTIONS

1. Place all ingredients except pita wedges and vegetables into slow cooker; stir to blend well. Cover; cook on LOW 2 hours.

2. Serve with pita wedges and vegetables. *Makes 4 cups dip*

Vegetable Hummus

2 cloves garlic
2 cans (15 to 19 ounces each) chick peas or garbanzo beans,
    rinsed and drained
1 package KNORR® Recipe Classics™ Vegetable Soup, Dip and
    Recipe Mix
½ cup water
½ cup BERTOLLI® Olive Oil
2 tablespoons lemon juice
¼ teaspoon ground cumin
6 (8-inch) whole wheat or white pita breads, cut into wedges

• In food processor, pulse garlic until finely chopped. Add remaining ingredients except pita bread. Process until smooth; chill at least 2 hours.

• Stir hummus before serving. If desired, add 1 to 2 tablespoons additional olive oil, or to taste. Serve with pita wedges. *Makes 3½ cups dip*

Prep Time: 10 minutes
Chill Time: 2 hours

Creamy Artichoke-Parmesan Dip

Festive Bacon & Cheese Dip

**2 packages (8 ounces each) cream cheese,
   softened and cut into cubes**
4 cups shredded Colby-Jack cheese
1 cup half-and-half
2 tablespoons prepared mustard
1 tablespoon chopped onion
2 teaspoons Worcestershire sauce
½ teaspoon salt
¼ teaspoon hot pepper sauce
1 pound bacon, cooked and crumbled

SLOW COOKER DIRECTIONS

Place cream cheese, Colby-Jack cheese, half-and-half, mustard, onion, Worcestershire sauce, salt and hot pepper sauce in slow cooker. Cover; cook on LOW 1 hour or until cheese melts, stirring occasionally. Stir in bacon; adjust seasonings, if desired. Serve with crusty bread or fruit and vegetable dippers. *Makes about 1 quart*

Ranch Bacon Cheddar Dip

2 packages (8 ounces each) cream cheese, softened
2 cups shredded Cheddar cheese (about 8 ounces)
¾ cup milk
1 envelope LIPTON® RECIPE SECRETS® Ranch Soup Mix
2 tablespoons bacon bits or crumbled bacon

1. Preheat oven to 325°F. In medium bowl, with electric mixer, beat cream cheese until smooth and fluffy, about 2 minutes. Stir in cheese, milk, soup mix and bacon bits.

2. Transfer to a lightly greased shallow 1-quart casserole. Bake, uncovered, 20 to 25 minutes or until heated through. Stir before serving.

3. Serve, if desired, with tortilla chips. *Makes 3 cups dip*

Prep Time: 5 minutes
Cook Time: 20 minutes

Festive Bacon & Cheese Dip

Three Mushroom Ratatouille

1 package (3½ ounces) fresh shiitake mushrooms*
1 tablespoon olive oil
1 large onion, chopped
4 cloves garlic, minced
1 package (8 ounces) button mushrooms, chopped
1 package (6 ounces) crimini mushrooms, chopped
1 cup chicken broth
½ cup chopped fresh tomato
2 tablespoons chopped fresh parsley
2 tablespoons grated Parmesan cheese
3 pita breads (6 inches each)
   Italian parsley for garnish

Or, substitute 1 ounce dried black Chinese mushrooms. Place dried mushrooms in small bowl; cover with warm water. Soak 20 minutes to soften. Drain; squeeze out excess moisture. Prepare as directed in Step 1.

1. Remove stems from shiitake mushrooms; discard stems and chop caps.

2. Preheat broiler. Heat oil in large skillet over medium heat until hot. Add onion and garlic. Cook 5 minutes, stirring occasionally. Add mushrooms; cook 5 minutes more, stirring often.

3. Add chicken broth; bring to a boil. Cook about 10 minutes or until liquid is absorbed. Remove from heat. Stir in tomato, parsley and cheese. Spoon into bowl.

4. Meanwhile, split each pita bread horizontally in half. Stack halves; cut stack into 6 wedges. Arrange wedges in single layer on baking sheet. Broil 4 inches from heat 1 to 3 minutes or until wedges are toasted.

5. Arrange toasted pita bread triangles and warm dip on serving platter. Garnish, if desired.

Makes about 2¼ cups

Three Mushroom Ratatouille

BLT Dip

1 envelope LIPTON® RECIPE SECRETS® Onion Soup Mix*
1 container (8 ounces) sour cream
1 cup HELLMANN'S® or BEST FOODS® Mayonnaise
1 medium tomato, chopped (about 1 cup)
½ cup cooked crumbled bacon (about 6 slices) or
  bacon bits
Shredded lettuce

*Also terrific with LIPTON® RECIPE SECRETS® Golden Onion Soup Mix.

1. In medium bowl, combine all ingredients except lettuce; chill if desired.

2. Garnish with lettuce and serve with your favorite dippers.

Makes 3 cups dip

Prep Time: 10 minutes

Hot Artichoke Dip

1 jar (1 pound) RAGÚ® Cheese Creations!® Classic Alfredo
  Sauce
1 package (8 ounces) cream cheese, softened
1 cup grated Parmesan cheese, divided
2 jars (6 ounces each) marinated artichoke hearts, drained
  and chopped

1. Preheat oven to 350°F. In medium bowl, with wire whisk or wooden spoon, thoroughly blend Ragú Cheese Creations! Sauce, cream cheese and ¾ cup Parmesan cheese. Stir in artichokes.

2. Turn into 1½-quart casserole and sprinkle with remaining ¼ cup Parmesan cheese.

3. Bake, uncovered, 25 minutes or until golden and heated through. Serve, if desired, with sliced Italian or French bread or crackers.   *Makes 4 cups dip*

Prep Time: 10 minutes
Cook Time: 25 minutes

Spicy Bavarian Dip

3 jalapeño peppers
3 cups water
1 (12-ounce) can tomato paste
4 teaspoons minced garlic, divided
1 teaspoon salt
1 teaspoon dried oregano leaves
1 teaspoon red pepper flakes
1 teaspoon ground cumin, divided
1 package BOB EVANS® Bratwurst (approximately 5 links)
½ teaspoon ground cinnamon
1 (14-ounce) can Bavarian sauerkraut, drained and finely
    chopped
Toasted pita points

Preheat oven to 400°F. Roast jalapeño peppers 4 minutes; chop finely. Combine water, tomato paste, 2 teaspoons garlic, salt, oregano, red pepper flakes and ½ teaspoon cumin in large saucepan. Add jalapeño peppers; cook over medium heat 10 minutes. Remove from heat.

Meanwhile, remove casing from bratwurst and cook in skillet until browned, breaking into small pieces. Stir in remaining 2 teaspoons garlic, ½ teaspoon cumin and cinnamon. Add bratwurst mixture and sauerkraut to saucepan; heat 3 minutes over medium heat. Serve dip hot with toasted pita points. Refrigerate leftovers. *Makes 10 to 12 servings*

Zesty Fun Pretzel Dip

½ cup *French's*® Bold n' Spicy Brown Mustard
½ cup honey

1. Combine mustard and honey.

2. Use for dipping pretzels, chips or cheese cubes. *Makes 1 cup*

Prep Time: 5 minutes

Ginger-Lemon Cheese Spread with Pineapple-Peach Sauce

2 packages (8 ounces each) cream cheese, softened
1 cup sour cream
3 tablespoons packed brown sugar
1 tablespoon grated lemon peel
¾ teaspoon ground ginger
½ cup crushed pineapple, well drained
½ cup peach or apricot preserves
Assorted crackers and fresh fruit

1. Line 3-cup decorative mold or bowl with plastic wrap.

2. Combine cream cheese and sour cream in large bowl; beat until creamy. (Do not overbeat.) Add brown sugar, lemon peel and ginger; stir until well blended.

3. Spoon cheese mixture into prepared mold. Cover with plastic wrap; refrigerate at least 8 hours or up to 2 days.

4. To complete recipe, combine pineapple and peach preserves in small bowl. Unmold cheese spread onto serving plate. Spoon sauce around cheese. Serve with crackers and fresh fruit.   *Makes 8 servings*

Variation: Press toasted chopped walnuts onto cheese spread and serve Pineapple-Peach Sauce alongside of spread.

Serving Suggestion: Serve cheese spread with assorted crackers and apple and pear slices.

Make-Ahead Time: Up to 2 days before serving
Final Prep Time: 5 minutes

DIPS & SPREADS

Ginger-Lemon Cheese Spread
with Pineapple-Peach Sauce

Chutney Cheese Spread

2 packages (8 ounces each) fat-free cream cheese, softened
1 cup (4 ounces) shredded reduced-fat Cheddar cheese
½ cup mango chutney
¼ cup thinly sliced green onions with tops
3 tablespoons dark raisins, chopped
2 cloves garlic, minced
1 to 1½ teaspoons curry powder
¾ teaspoon ground coriander
½ to ¾ teaspoon ground ginger
1 tablespoon chopped dry roasted peanuts

1. Place cream cheese and Cheddar cheese in food processor or blender; process until smooth. Stir in chutney, green onions, raisins, garlic, curry powder, coriander and ginger. Cover; refrigerate 2 to 3 hours.

2. Top spread with peanuts. Serve with additional green onions and melba toast, if desired. *Makes 20 servings*

Variation: The spread may also be garnished with one tablespoon toasted coconut to provide a slightly sweeter flavor.

Herbed Garlic & Artichoke Dip

1 (6.5-ounce) package ALOUETTE® Garlic & Herbs or Light Garlic & Herbs
1 (15-ounce) can artichoke hearts, drained and chopped
½ cup minced green onions
2 tablespoons chopped sun-dried tomatoes
Freshly ground black pepper to taste

Preheat oven to 375°F.

Blend Alouette, artichokes, onions, tomatoes and pepper. Place cheese mixture in 2-cup oven-to-table dish; bake 10 to 12 minutes or until brown and bubbly. Serve warm with breadsticks, crackers or raw vegetables.

Makes 2 cups dip

Chutney Cheese Spread

Five-Layered Mexican Dip

½ **cup low-fat sour cream**
½ **cup GUILTLESS GOURMET® Salsa (Roasted Red Pepper**
   or Southwestern Grill)
1 **jar (16 ounces) GUILTLESS GOURMET® Black Bean Dip**
   (Spicy or Mild)
2 **cups shredded lettuce**
½ **cup chopped tomato**
¼ **cup (1 ounce) shredded sharp Cheddar cheese**
   Chopped fresh cilantro and cilantro sprigs (optional)
1 **large bag (7 ounces) GUILTLESS GOURMET® Baked Tortilla**
   Chips (yellow, white or blue corn)

Mix together sour cream and salsa in small bowl. Spread bean dip in shallow glass bowl. Top with sour cream-salsa mixture, spreading to cover bean dip.* Just before serving, top with lettuce, tomato and cheese. Garnish with cilantro, if desired. Serve with tortilla chips.   *Makes 8 servings*

*Dip may be prepared to this point; cover and refrigerate up to 24 hours.

Chili Dip

1 **container (16 ounces) sour cream**
1 **medium tomato, chopped (about 1 cup)**
1 **can (4 ounces) chopped green chilies, drained**
1 **package KNORR® Recipe Classics™ Leek Soup,**
   Dip and Recipe Mix
3 **to 4 teaspoons chili powder**

• In medium bowl, combine all ingredients; chill at least 2 hours.

• Stir before serving. Serve with corn chips or cut-up vegetables.
                                                  Makes about 3 cups dip

Cheese Chili Dip: Stir in 1 cup shredded Monterey Jack cheese (about 4 ounces).

Variation: Use this dip to make Tortilla Roll-Ups. Simply spread Chili Dip on flour tortillas, top with cut-up cooked chicken, roll up and serve.

Prep Time: 5 minutes
Chill Time: 2 hours

Five-Layered Mexican Dip

Nutty Broccoli Spread

1 box (10 ounces) BIRDS EYE® frozen Chopped Broccoli
4 ounces cream cheese
¼ cup grated Parmesan cheese
1 teaspoon dried basil
¼ cup walnuts
1 loaf frozen garlic bread

• Cook broccoli according to package directions; drain well.

• Preheat oven to 400°F. Place broccoli, cream cheese, Parmesan cheese and basil in food processor or blender; process until ingredients are mixed. (Do not overmix.) Add walnuts; process 3 to 5 seconds.

• Split garlic bread lengthwise. Spread broccoli mixture evenly over bread.

• Bake 10 to 15 minutes or until bread is toasted and broccoli mixture is heated through.

• Cut bread into slices; serve hot. *Makes about 2 cups spread*

Prep Time: 10 minutes
Cook Time: 10 to 15 minutes

Two Cheese Pesto Dip

1 cup light sour cream
½ cup (2 ounces) SARGENTO® Light Mozzarella Shredded Cheese
½ cup light mayonnaise
½ cup finely chopped fresh parsley
¼ cup finely chopped walnuts
2 tablespoons SARGENTO® Fancy Parmesan Shredded Cheese
1½ teaspoons dried basil leaves *or* 3 tablespoons minced fresh basil
1 clove garlic, minced

Combine all ingredients in medium bowl. Cover and refrigerate several hours or overnight. Garnish with whole walnuts, if desired. Serve with assorted fresh vegetables. *Makes 2 cups*

Nutty Broccoli Spread

Party Pizza Spread

2 **packages (8 ounces each) cream cheese, softened**
1 **packet (1 ounce) HIDDEN VALLEY® The Original Ranch®**
   Salad Dressing & Seasoning Mix
½ **teaspoon minced garlic**
½ **teaspoon dried rosemary, crushed**
1 **cup chili sauce**
½ **cup chopped green onions**
1 **cup shredded Monterey Jack cheese**
½ **cup mushroom slices, olives, ham, green pepper, or any**
   favorite pizza topping

In large bowl, blend cream cheese, salad dressing & seasoning mix, garlic and rosemary until smooth. Spread into 10-inch circle on serving platter, smoothing mixture with spatula. Pour chili sauce over cream cheese mixture into 9-inch circle, creating "cheese crust" border. Sprinkle with green onions, cheese and toppings. Refrigerate at least 30 minutes before serving. Serve with crackers for dipping. *Makes 8 to 10 servings*

Pineapple-Almond Cheese Spread

2 **cans (8 ounces each) DOLE® Crushed Pineapple**
1 **package (8 ounces) cream cheese, softened**
4 **cups (16 ounces) shredded sharp Cheddar cheese**
½ **cup mayonnaise**
1 **tablespoon soy sauce**
1 **cup chopped natural almonds, toasted**
½ **cup finely chopped DOLE® Green Bell Pepper**
¼ **cup minced green onions or chives**
   DOLE® Celery stalks or assorted breads

Drain crushed pineapple. In large bowl, beat cream cheese until smooth; beat in Cheddar cheese, mayonnaise and soy sauce until smooth. Stir in crushed pineapple, almonds, green pepper and onions. Refrigerate, covered. Use to stuff celery stalks or serve as spread with assorted breads. Serve at room temperature. *Makes 4 cups*

Hummus Vegetable Dip

1 (16-ounce) can chick-peas, rinsed and well drained
5 tablespoons lemon juice
¼ cup water
¼ cup tahini (sesame seed paste)
2 tablespoons FILIPPO BERIO® Olive Oil
1 to 2 cloves garlic, sliced
¼ teaspoon ground cumin
 Salt and freshly ground black pepper
 Few drops hot pepper sauce (optional)
 Additional lemon juice (optional)
 Assorted cut-up fresh vegetables
 Pita bread wedges
 Oil-cured black olives (optional)
 Additional FILIPPO BERIO® Olive Oil (optional)

In blender container or food processor, place chick-peas, 5 tablespoons lemon juice, water, tahini, 2 tablespoons olive oil, garlic and cumin; process until mixture is thick and creamy. Season to taste with salt, black pepper and hot pepper sauce, if desired. Adjust consistency with additional lemon juice or water, if desired. Transfer to serving bowl. Cover; refrigerate at least 1 hour before serving. Serve with vegetables and pita bread; garnish dip with olives and drizzle of additional olive oil, if desired.   *Makes about 1¼ cups dip*

Pepper and Parsley Logs

1 packet (1 ounce) HIDDEN VALLEY® The Original Ranch®
  Salad Dressing & Seasoning Mix
8 ounces cream cheese, softened
2 teaspoons cracked black pepper
2 teaspoons chopped fresh parsley

Combine dressing mix and cream cheese. Divide in half; chill until firm. Roll into two 1½-inch logs, coating one with pepper and the other with parsley. Wrap in plastic wrap; chill.   *Makes 2 logs*

Serving Suggestion: Spread on crackers or bread.

White Pizza Dip

**1 envelope LIPTON® RECIPE SECRETS® Savory Herb
   with Garlic Soup Mix**
1 container (16 ounces) sour cream
1 cup (8 ounces) ricotta cheese
1 cup shredded mozzarella cheese (about 4 ounces), divided
¼ cup (1 ounce) chopped pepperoni (optional)
1 loaf Italian or French bread, sliced

1. Preheat oven to 350°F. In shallow 1-quart casserole, combine soup mix, sour cream, ricotta cheese, ¾ cup mozzarella cheese and pepperoni.

2. Sprinkle with remaining ¼ cup mozzarella cheese.

3. Bake, uncovered, 30 minutes or until heated through. Serve with bread.

Makes 3 cups dip

Prep Time: 10 minutes
Cook Time: 30 minutes

Savory Peanut Butter Dip

¼ cup creamy peanut butter
3 ounces fat-free cream cheese
1 to 2 tablespoons lemon or apple juice
½ teaspoon ground cinnamon
⅛ to ¼ cup natural applesauce
2 apples, sliced
1 small banana, sliced
Celery stalks, sliced into 4-inch pieces
2 cups broccoli flowerets

Combine the peanut butter, cream cheese, juice and cinnamon in food processor. Blend until smooth. Add applesauce, little by little, to bring to the desired consistency for the dip. Chill before serving with fresh fruits or vegetables.

Makes about 8 servings

*Favorite recipe from **Peanut Advisory Board***

White Pizza Dip

Cheesy Mustard Dip

1 container (8 ounces) whipped cream cheese
¼ cup milk
3 tablespoons *French's®* Bold n' Spicy Brown Mustard
  or Sweet & Tangy Honey Mustard
2 tablespoons mayonnaise
2 tablespoons minced green onions

Combine ingredients for dip in medium bowl; mix until well blended.

Makes 8 servings (about 1¼ cups dip)

Prep Time: 15 minutes

Tex Mex Hot Dip

1 pound BOB EVANS® Original Recipe Roll Sausage
½ cup chopped onion
⅓ cup chopped bell pepper (red, yellow or green)
½ cup diced fresh tomato
¼ cup chopped fresh cilantro
1 (4-ounce) can chili peppers, drained and chopped
1 teaspoon hot pepper sauce
½ teaspoon ground cumin
½ teaspoon chili powder
2 cups (8 ounces) shredded Monterey Jack cheese
2 cups (8 ounces) shredded Cheddar cheese
1 (14-ounce) bag corn tortilla chips

Preheat oven to 350°F. Cook sausage, onion and bell pepper in large skillet until sausage is browned; drain on paper towels. Place in 2-quart casserole dish. Stir in tomato, cilantro, chili peppers, hot pepper sauce, cumin and chili powder. Top with cheeses; bake, uncovered, 10 to 15 minutes or until dip is heated through and cheese is melted. Serve with tortilla chips. Refrigerate leftovers.

Makes 10 to 12 servings

Cheesy Mustard Dip; Zesty Fun Pretzel
Dip (page 59); French's® Honey Mustard

Celebration Cheese Ball

2 packages (8 ounces) cream cheese, softened
⅓ cup mayonnaise
¼ cup grated Parmesan cheese
2 tablespoons finely chopped carrot
1 tablespoon finely chopped red onion
1½ teaspoons prepared horseradish
¼ teaspoon salt
½ cup chopped pecans or walnuts
Assorted crackers and breadsticks

Blend all ingredients except pecans and crackers in medium bowl. Cover and refrigerate until firm.

Form cheese mixture into a ball; roll in pecans. Wrap cheese ball in plastic wrap and refrigerate at least 1 hour. Serve with assorted crackers and breadsticks.

Makes about 2½ cups

Roasted Eggplant Dip

2 medium eggplants, about 1 pound each
1 package KNORR® Recipe Classics™ Roasted Garlic Herb Soup, Dip and Recipe Mix
⅓ to ½ cup BERTOLLI® Olive Oil
2 tablespoons lemon juice
¼ cup chopped fresh parsley
6 (8-inch) whole wheat or white pita breads, cut into wedges

• Preheat oven to 400°F. Cut eggplants lengthwise in half. Arrange eggplants in foil-lined baking pan. Bake 50 minutes or until very tender; cool.

• With spoon, scrape eggplant from skins and place in food processor.* Add recipe mix, oil and lemon juice. Process until smooth; chill 2 hours.

• Stir in parsley just before serving. Serve with pita wedges.

Makes 2 cups dip

Or, chop on cutting board with knife.

Celebration Cheese Ball

Hot Broccoli Dip

1 container (16 ounces) sour cream
½ cup HELLMANN'S® or BEST FOODS® Mayonnaise
⅓ cup grated Parmesan cheese (about 1½ ounces)
**1 package (10 ounces) frozen chopped broccoli, thawed
  and squeezed dry**
**1 package KNORR® Recipe Classics™ Vegetable Soup, Dip
  and Recipe Mix**
⅛ teaspoon hot pepper sauce

• Preheat oven to 350°F. In medium bowl, blend all ingredients. Spoon into shallow baking dish. If desired, sprinkle with additional Parmesan cheese.

• Bake 35 to 40 minutes or until edges are golden brown and bubbly. Serve with crackers. *Makes about 3½ cups dip*

Microwave Directions: In medium bowl, blend all ingredients; spoon into microwavable dish. Microwave at HIGH (100%) Full Power 3 minutes. Stir and microwave 3 to 4 minutes or until hot and bubbling.

Prep Time: 5 minutes
Cook Time: 35 minutes

Pepperoni Pizza Dip

1 cup RAGÚ® Old World Style® Pasta Sauce
1 cup RAGÚ® Cheese Creations!® Classic Alfredo Sauce
1 cup shredded mozzarella cheese (about 4 ounces)
¼ to ½ cup finely chopped pepperoni

1. In 2-quart saucepan, heat Ragú Pasta Sauces, cheese and pepperoni, stirring occasionally, 10 minutes or until cheese is melted.

2. Pour into 1½-quart casserole or serving dish. Serve, if desired, with breadsticks, sliced Italian bread or crackers. *Makes 3½ cups dip*

Prep Time: 5 minutes
Cook Time: 10 minutes

Maple-Glazed Meatballs

Honey-Mustard Chicken Wings

3 **pounds chicken wings**
1 **teaspoon salt**
1 **teaspoon black pepper**
½ **cup honey**
½ **cup barbecue sauce**
2 **tablespoons spicy brown mustard**
1 **clove garlic, minced**
3 **to 4 thin lemon slices**

SLOW COOKER DIRECTIONS

1. Rinse chicken and pat dry. Cut off wing tips; discard. Cut each wing at joint to make two pieces. Sprinkle salt and pepper on both sides of chicken. Place wing pieces on broiler rack. Broil 4 to 5 inches from heat about 10 minutes, turning halfway through cooking. Place broiled chicken wings in slow cooker.

2. Combine honey, barbecue sauce, mustard and garlic in small bowl; mix well. Pour sauce over chicken wings. Top with lemon slices. Cover; cook on LOW 4 to 5 hours.

3. Remove and discard lemon slices. Serve wings with sauce.

Makes about 24 appetizers

Prep Time: 20 minutes
Cook Time: 4 to 5 hours

Sausage Cheese Puffs

1 **pound BOB EVANS® Original Recipe Roll Sausage**
2½ **cups (10 ounces) shredded sharp Cheddar cheese**
2 **cups biscuit mix**
½ **cup water**
1 **teaspoon baking powder**

Preheat oven to 350°F. Combine ingredients in large bowl until blended. Shape into 1-inch balls. Place on lightly greased baking sheets. Bake about 25 minutes or until golden brown. Serve hot. Refrigerate leftovers.

Makes about 60 appetizers

Honey-Mustard Chicken Wings

Tortilla Pizzettes

1 cup chunky salsa
1 cup refried beans
2 tablespoons chopped fresh cilantro
½ teaspoon ground cumin
3 large (10-inch) flour tortillas
1 cup (4 ounces) shredded Mexican cheese blend

Pour salsa into strainer; let drain at least 20 minutes.

Meanwhile, combine refried beans, cilantro and cumin in small bowl; mix well. Preheat oven to 400°F. Spray baking sheet lightly with nonstick cooking spray; set aside.

Cut each tortilla into 2½-inch circles with round cookie cutter (9 to 10 circles per tortilla). Spread each tortilla circle with refried bean mixture, leaving ¼ inch around edge. Top each with heaping teaspoon drained salsa; sprinkle with about 1 teaspoon cheese.

Place pizzettes on prepared baking sheet. Bake about 7 minutes or until tortillas are golden brown. *Makes about 30 pizzettes*

Nacho Bacho

1½ pounds ground beef
1 cup chunky hot salsa
½ cup salad dressing
2 tablespoons Italian seasoning
1 tablespoon chili powder
2 cups (8 ounces) shredded Colby-Jack cheese, divided
3 cups nacho-flavored tortilla chips, crushed
1 cup sour cream
½ cup sliced black olives

Brown ground beef; drain. In medium bowl, combine salsa, salad dressing, Italian seasoning and chili powder. Add beef. Place in 11×7-inch baking dish. Top with 1 cup cheese. Cover with crushed chips and remaining 1 cup cheese. Bake at 350°F 20 minutes. Garnish with sour cream and sliced olives.

Makes 8 to 12 appetizer servings

*Favorite recipe from **North Dakota Beef Commission***

Roasted Red Pepper and Artichoke Torte

2½ cups chopped bagels (about 3 bagels)
2 tablespoons olive oil
    Vegetable cooking spray
2 packages (8 ounces each) cream cheese, softened
1 container (15 ounces) ricotta cheese
1 can (10¾ ounces) condensed cream of celery soup
1 container (4 ounces) cholesterol-free egg substitute
    (equivalent to 2 eggs)
2 tablespoons chopped green onion
1 tablespoon dried Italian seasoning
1 clove garlic, minced
1 can (8½ ounces) artichoke hearts, drained and chopped
1 jar (15 ounces) roasted red bell peppers, drained and
    chopped, divided
1 cup chopped fresh basil, divided

In medium bowl, combine bagels and oil; mix well. Spray 9×2½-inch springform baking pan with vegetable cooking spray. Press bagel mixture into bottom of springform pan. Bake at 375°F 15 minutes; cool.

With electric mixer, combine cheeses, soup, egg substitute, green onion, Italian seasoning and garlic; mix well. Spread half of cheese mixture over bagel crust. Top with artichokes and half each of peppers and basil. Spread remaining cheese filling over basil; top with remaining peppers. Bake at 375°F 1 hour or until set in middle; cool. Refrigerate 6 to 8 hours or overnight. Run knife around edge of torte; remove side of pan. Top with remaining basil. Slice thinly and serve with crackers. *Makes 20 servings*

Roasted Red Pepper and Artichoke Torte

Holiday Appetizer Quiche

CRUST
- 2 cups all-purpose flour
- 1 teaspoon salt
- ¾ Butter Flavor CRISCO® Stick or ¾ cup Butter Flavor CRISCO® all-vegetable shortening plus additional for shortening
- 5 tablespoons cold water

FILLING
- 2 cups (8 ounces) shredded Swiss cheese
- ⅔ cup chopped ham, crumbled cooked sausage, diced pepperoni or crumbled cooked bacon
- ¾ cup thinly sliced green onions (including tops)
- ¼ cup snipped fresh parsley
- 1 jar (4 ounces) diced pimientos, well drained
- 5 eggs
- 1 cup whipping cream
- 1 cup half-and-half
- 1 teaspoon salt
- ¼ teaspoon pepper

1. Heat oven to 400°F.

2. For crust, combine flour and salt in medium bowl. Cut in ¾ cup shortening using pastry blender (or 2 knives) until all flour is blended in to form pea-size chunks. Sprinkle with water, 1 tablespoon at a time. Toss lightly with fork until dough forms ball.

3. Roll out dough to fit 15×10-inch jelly-roll pan. Place dough in greased pan, folding edges under. Flute edges. Prick crust with fork.

4. For filling, sprinkle cheese, ham, onions, parsley and pimientos evenly over crust. Beat eggs, cream, half-and-half, salt and pepper in medium bowl. Pour over filled crust.

5. Bake at 400°F for 25 to 30 minutes or until set. *Do not overbake.* Cool 5 to 10 minutes. Cut into 2×1½-inch pieces. Serve warm.

Makes about 50 appetizers

Note: Crust may bubble during baking and need to be pricked with fork again.

I Have to Bring Something!!
Turkey Roll-Ups

1 package (6 ounces) BUTTERBALL® Fat Free Oven Roasted Deli-Thin Sliced Turkey Breast
1 container (8 ounces) soft cream cheese
½ cup prepared medium-hot salsa
2 green onions, chopped
2 tablespoons minced fresh cilantro
6 (10-inch) flour tortillas
1 red bell pepper, cut into strips
2 cups shredded lettuce

Combine cream cheese, salsa, onions and cilantro in medium bowl. Spread cream cheese mixture on tortillas; top with turkey slices. Place bell pepper and lettuce on turkey. Roll tortillas into pinwheels. Cut each pinwheel into fourths. *Makes 24 appetizers*

Prep Time: 15 minutes

Sensational Stuffed Mushrooms

30 large mushrooms (about 1 pound)
½ pound bulk pork sausage
1 cup chopped dried tart cherries
1 (8-ounce) package cream cheese, softened
2 green onions, sliced

Pull stems from mushrooms and discard (or save for another use). Rinse mushroom caps; drain well. Set aside.

Cook sausage in large skillet, stirring to break up meat, 5 minutes or until sausage is done. Remove from heat. Add dried cherries, cream cheese and onions; mix well. Fill each mushroom cap with heaping teaspoonful of sausage mixture.

Place filled mushrooms on a lightly greased baking sheet. Bake in a preheated 425°F oven 6 to 8 minutes. Serve immediately. *Makes 30 appetizers*

*Favorite recipe from **Cherry Marketing Institute***

Jerk Wings
with Ranch Dipping Sauce

- ½ **cup mayonnaise**
- ½ **cup plain yogurt or sour cream**
- 1½ **teaspoons salt, divided**
- 1¼ **teaspoons garlic powder, divided**
- ½ **teaspoon black pepper, divided**
- ¼ **teaspoon onion powder**
- 2 **tablespoons orange juice**
- 1 **teaspoon sugar**
- 1 **teaspoon dried thyme leaves**
- 1 **teaspoon paprika**
- ¼ **teaspoon ground nutmeg**
- ¼ **teaspoon ground red pepper**
- 2½ **pounds chicken wings (about 10 wings)**

For Ranch Dipping Sauce, combine mayonnaise, yogurt, ½ teaspoon salt, ¼ teaspoon garlic powder, ¼ teaspoon black pepper and onion powder in small bowl.

Preheat oven to 450°F.

Combine orange juice, sugar, thyme, paprika, nutmeg, red pepper, remaining 1 teaspoon salt, 1 teaspoon garlic powder and ¼ teaspoon black pepper in small bowl.

Cut tips from wings; discard. Place wings in large bowl. Drizzle with orange juice mixture; toss to coat.

Transfer chicken to greased broiler pan. Bake 25 to 30 minutes or until juices run clear and skin is crisp. Serve with Ranch Dipping Sauce.

Makes 6 to 7 servings

Serving Suggestion: Serve with celery sticks.

Jerk Wings with Ranch Dipping Sauce

Easy Spinach Appetizer

2 **tablespoons butter**
1 **cup milk**
3 **eggs**
1 **cup all-purpose flour**
1 **teaspoon baking powder**
1 **teaspoon salt**
4 **cups (16 ounces) shredded Monterey Jack cheese**
2 **packages (10 ounces each) frozen chopped spinach,**
   thawed and well drained
½ **cup diced red bell pepper**

Preheat oven to 350°F. Melt butter in 13×9-inch pan.

Beat milk, eggs, flour, baking powder and salt in medium bowl until well blended. Stir in cheese, spinach and bell pepper; mix well. Spread mixture over melted butter in pan.

Bake 40 to 45 minutes or until firm. Let stand 10 minutes before cutting into triangles or squares. *Makes 2 to 4 dozen pieces*

TIP Make these appetizers ahead of time for last minute gatherings. Mix and bake as directed above. Transfer squares to a cookie sheet; place the cookie sheet in the freezer until the squares are frozen solid. Then transfer the squares to a resealable plastic food storage bag. Seal tightly and store in freezer. To serve, reheat squares in 325°F oven for 15 minutes.

Easy Spinach Appetizer

Barbecue Pizza

2 teaspoons olive oil
1 boneless skinless chicken breast (about 5 ounces), cut into
   ¾-inch cubes
3 ounces HILLSHIRE FARM® Pepperoni, sliced
⅓ cup barbecue sauce, divided
1 (12-inch) prepared pizza crust
1¼ cups shredded mozzarella cheese, divided
2 tablespoons thinly sliced green onion tops

Preheat oven to 450°F.

Heat oil in small skillet over medium-high heat. Sauté chicken until barely
done, 3 to 5 minutes. Remove from heat and pour off juices. Add Pepperoni
and 1 tablespoon barbecue sauce to chicken. Stir to mix and separate slices.

Spread remaining barbecue sauce over pizza crust. Sprinkle ¾ cup cheese over
sauce. Sprinkle pepperoni mixture over cheese; sprinkle with green onion. Top
with remaining ½ cup cheese. Place in oven directly on oven rack. Bake 8 to
10 minutes or until cheese is bubbly and pizza crust is crisp.

Makes 8 to 12 appetizer servings

Walnut Chicken Pinwheels

2 boneless skinless chicken breasts, halved
12 to 14 spinach leaves
1 package (6.5 ounces) ALOUETTE® Garlic & Herbs Cheese
5 ounces roasted red peppers, sliced or 5 ounces pimiento
   slices
¾ cup finely chopped California walnuts

Pound chicken to about ¼-inch thickness with flat side of meat mallet or
chef's knife. Cover each chicken piece with spinach leaves. Spread each with
Alouette®. Top with pepper slices and walnuts. Carefully roll up each breast
and secure with wooden toothpicks. Bake at 400°F 20 to 25 minutes until
cooked through. Chill. Remove toothpicks before serving, then slice into
½-inch rounds. Serve cold.

Makes about 35 appetizers

Barbecue Pizza

Devilish Crab Puffs

Swiss Puffs (recipe follows)
2 cups crabmeat, cleaned
¼ cup chopped fresh parsley
¼ cup mayonnaise
2 tablespoons finely minced onion
2 teaspoons white wine
1 teaspoon Worcestershire sauce
1 teaspoon dry mustard
1 teaspoon lemon juice
¼ teaspoon white pepper

1. Prepare Swiss Puffs; set aside.

2. To make filling, place crabmeat in medium bowl. Add parsley, mayonnaise, onion, wine, Worcestershire, mustard, lemon juice and pepper. Stir gently to blend.

3. Preheat oven to 375°F. Fill Swiss Puffs with crab filling.

4. Place filled appetizers on *ungreased* baking sheet; bake 10 minutes or until heated through. *Makes about 40 appetizers*

Swiss Puffs

½ cup milk
½ cup water
¼ cup butter or margarine
¼ teaspoon salt
Pinch ground nutmeg
Pinch white pepper
1 cup all-purpose flour
4 eggs, at room temperature
1 cup shredded, Swiss cheese, divided

1. Preheat oven to 400°F.

2. Heat milk, water, butter, salt, nutmeg and pepper in 3-quart saucepan over medium-high heat until mixture boils. Remove pan from heat; add flour, mixing until smooth. Cook over medium-low heat, stirring constantly, until mixture leaves side of pan clean and forms a ball. Remove pan from heat.

continued on page 96

Devilish Crab Puffs

3. Add eggs, 1 at a time, beating until smooth and shiny after each addition. Continue beating until mixture loses its gloss. Stir in ¾ cup cheese.

4. Drop rounded teaspoonfuls of cheese batter 1 inch apart onto 2 large greased baking sheets. Sprinkle with remaining ¼ cup cheese.

5. Bake 30 to 35 minutes or until puffs are golden brown. Cool completely on wire racks.

6. Before filling, cut tops off puffs; scoop out and discard moist dough in centers. *Makes about 4 dozen*

Roasted Vegetable Cheese Crispies

12 ounces shredded JARLSBERG LITE™ Cheese
1½ teaspoons dried thyme leaves
½ teaspoon dry mustard
½ teaspoon finely ground black pepper
1 large peeled potato
½ small peeled turnip
2 to 3 medium peeled carrots
8 to 10 small (or 4 to 5 large) peeled, thinly sliced shallots
**   or other mild flavored onion (1½ cups)**
6 large cloves garlic, minced
½ cup broth or water

Preheat oven to 425°F. Line 17×11-inch baking pan with foil. Coat with nonstick cooking spray.

Combine cheese, thyme, mustard and pepper in bowl and mix well, set aside.

Using slicing side of grater (or slicing disk of food processor), cut potato, turnip and carrot in nearly paper-thin slices. Mix vegetables with shallots and garlic and spread on bottom of baking pan.

Cover with cheese mixture; drizzle with broth. Bake 40 minutes. Cut into squares and serve hot or warm. Vegetables should be crisp on bottom, soft in middle and cheese crisp on top. *Makes 72 bite-size appetizer squares*

Chicken-Rice Roll Ups

 2 **cups finely chopped cooked chicken**
 2 **cups cooked rice**
 1 **can (8 ounces) water chestnuts, drained and finely chopped**
 1 **cup (4 ounces) shredded Cheddar cheese**
 1 **cup chopped celery**
 ⅔ **cup sour cream**
 ½ **cup finely chopped onion**
 1 **can (4 ounces) diced green chiles**
 2 **teaspoons chili powder**
 1 **teaspoon salt**
 ¼ **teaspoon hot pepper sauce**
66 **wonton skins**
 4 **cups vegetable oil for frying**
   Picante sauce

Combine chicken, rice, water chestnuts, cheese, celery, sour cream, onion, chiles, chili powder, salt and pepper sauce in large bowl. Place 1 tablespoon rice mixture in center of each wonton skin. Fold bottom corner up over filling, then fold in side corners over filling. Brush edges with water and roll up to seal. Heat oil in deep fryer or heavy saucepan to 375°F; fry rolls, a few at a time, 1 minute or until golden brown. Remove with slotted spoon; drain on paper towels. Serve warm with picante sauce for dipping.

Makes 66 appetizers

*Favorite recipe from **USA Rice Federation***

Cheesy Snack Squares

1¼ cups all-purpose flour
¾ cup cornmeal
2 medium green onions, thinly sliced
4 teaspoons sugar
2 teaspoons baking powder
1 teaspoon dried Italian seasonings
¼ teaspoon salt
1 cup milk
¼ cup vegetable oil
1 egg
1 cup (4 ounces) shredded Cheddar cheese
¼ cup finely chopped green bell pepper
¼ cup finely chopped red bell pepper
2 slices crisp-cooked bacon, crumbled

Preheat oven to 400°F. Grease 11×7-inch baking dish.

Combine flour, cornmeal, green onions, sugar, baking powder, Italian seasonings and salt in large bowl; mix well. Combine milk, oil and egg in small bowl. Add to cornmeal mixture; mix just until moistened. Spread evenly in prepared dish. Combine cheese, bell peppers and bacon in medium bowl. Sprinkle evenly over cornmeal mixture.

Bake 25 to 30 minutes or until wooden toothpick inserted into center comes out clean. Let stand 10 minutes before cutting.

Makes about 15 appetizers

Cheesy Snack Squares

Swedish-Style Meatballs

- **4 tablespoons butter or margarine, divided**
- **1 cup minced onion**
- **1 pound 90% lean ground beef**
- **½ pound ground veal**
- **½ pound ground pork**
- **1 cup fresh bread crumbs**
- **2 eggs, lightly beaten**
- **½ teaspoon salt**
- **¼ teaspoon black pepper**
- **⅛ teaspoon grated nutmeg**
- **3 tablespoons all-purpose flour**
- **1¼ cups milk**
- **¼ cup half-and-half**
- **1 egg yolk**
- **½ teaspoon salt**

Melt 2 tablespoons butter in large skillet over medium heat. Add onion. Cook and stir 8 to 10 minutes or until onions are very soft. Remove from heat and set aside. Combine beef, veal, pork, bread crumbs, beaten eggs, salt, pepper and nutmeg in large bowl. Add onions; mix well. Shape into balls (use 2 tablespoons of meat mixture for dinner-sized meatball or 1 tablespoon for cocktail-sized). Set aside.

Preheat oven to 200°F.

Reheat skillet over medium heat. Add ¼ to ⅓ of meatballs. *Do not crowd pan.* Cook 8 minutes, shaking pan to allow meatballs to roll and brown evenly. Reduce heat to medium-low. Cook 15 to 20 minutes or until cooked through. Transfer to covered casserole dish and keep warm in oven.

Meanwhile, wipe out skillet. Melt remaining 2 tablespoons butter over medium heat. Whisk in flour. Stir well. Combine milk, half-and-half, egg yolk and salt in small bowl. Slowly stir into flour mixture. Reduce heat to medium-low. Cook and stir 3 minutes or until thickened. Remove dish from oven and pour sauce over meatballs. Serve immediately.

Makes 72 cocktail-size meatballs

Chicken Pesto Pizza

1 loaf (1 pound) frozen bread dough, thawed
8 ounces chicken tenders, cut into ½-inch pieces
½ red onion, cut into quarters and thinly sliced
¼ cup prepared pesto
2 large plum tomatoes, seeded and diced
1 cup (4 ounces) shredded pizza cheese blend or
    mozzarella cheese

Preheat oven to 375°F. Roll out bread dough on floured surface to 14×8-inch rectangle. Transfer to baking sheet sprinkled with cornmeal. Cover loosely with plastic wrap and let rise 20 to 30 minutes.

Meanwhile, spray large skillet with nonstick cooking spray; heat over medium heat. Add chicken; cook and stir 2 minutes. Add onion and pesto; cook and stir 3 to 4 minutes or until chicken is cooked through. Stir in tomatoes; remove from heat and let cool slightly.

Spread chicken mixture evenly over bread dough within 1 inch of edges. Sprinkle with cheese.

Bake on bottom rack of oven about 20 minutes or until crust is golden brown. Cut into 2-inch squares. *Makes about 20 appetizer pieces*

Original Ranch® Drummettes

1 packet (1 ounce) HIDDEN VALLEY® The Original Ranch®
    Salad Dressing & Seasoning Mix
¼ cup vegetable oil
24 chicken drummettes (about 2 pounds)

Combine dressing mix and oil in large bowl. Add drummettes; toss well to coat. Arrange on rack placed in foil-lined baking pan; bake at 425°F for 25 minutes. Turn drummettes over; bake additional 20 minutes.
Makes 24 drummettes

Spicy Hot Variation: Add 2 tablespoons red pepper sauce to dressing mixture before coating.

Serving Suggestion: Dip cooked drummettes in prepared Hidden Valley® Original Ranch® Salad Dressing.

Chicken Pesto Pizza

Stuffed Party Baguette

2 medium red bell peppers
1 French bread loaf, about 14 inches long
¼ cup plus 2 tablespoons prepared fat-free Italian dressing, divided
1 small red onion, very thinly sliced
8 large fresh basil leaves
3 ounces Swiss cheese, very thinly sliced

1. Preheat oven to 425°F. Cover large baking sheet with foil.

2. To roast bell peppers, cut peppers in half; remove stems, seeds and membranes. Place peppers, cut sides down, on prepared baking sheet. Bake 20 to 25 minutes or until skins are browned, turning occasionally.

3. Transfer peppers from baking sheet to paper bag; close bag tightly. Let stand 10 minutes or until peppers are cool enough to handle and skins are loosened. Peel off skins using sharp knife; discard skins. Cut peppers into strips.

4. Trim ends from bread; discard. Cut loaf lengthwise in half. Remove soft insides of loaf; reserve removed bread for another use.

5. Brush ¼ cup Italian dressing evenly onto cut sides of bread. Arrange pepper strips in even layer in bottom half of loaf; top with even layer of onion. Brush onion with remaining 2 tablespoons Italian dressing; top with layer of basil and cheese. Replace bread top. Wrap loaf tightly in heavy-duty plastic wrap; refrigerate at least 2 hours or overnight.

6. When ready to serve, cut loaf crosswise into 1-inch slices. Secure with wooden picks and garnish, if desired. *Makes 12 servings*

Stuffed Party Baguette

Cheese & Sausage Bundles

    Salsa (recipe follows)
  ¼ pound bulk hot Italian pork sausage
  1 cup (4 ounces) shredded Monterey Jack cheese
  1 can (4 ounces) chopped green chilies
  2 tablespoons finely chopped green onion
40 wonton wrappers
  1 quart vegetable oil for deep frying

1. Prepare Salsa; set aside and keep warm. Brown sausage in small skillet over medium-high heat 6 to 8 minutes, stirring to separate meat. Drain off drippings. Combine sausage, cheese, chilies and onion in medium bowl. Spoon 1 round teaspoon sausage mixture near 1 corner of wonton wrapper. Brush opposite corner with water. Fold over corner; roll up jelly-roll style.

2. Moisten ends of roll with water. Bring ends together to make a "bundle," overlapping ends slightly; firmly press to seal. Repeat with remaining filling and wonton wrappers.

3. Heat oil in heavy 3-quart saucepan over medium heat until deep-fat thermometer registers 365°F. Fry bundles, a few at a time, about 1½ minutes or until golden. Adjust heat to maintain temperature. (Allow oil to return to 365°F between batches.) Drain on paper towels. Serve with Salsa.

Makes 40 appetizers

Salsa

1 can (16 ounces) whole tomatoes, undrained
2 tablespoons olive oil
2 tablespoons chopped green onion
2 cloves garlic, minced
3 tablespoons chopped fresh cilantro or parsley

Combine tomatoes with juice and oil in food processor; process until chopped. Pour into 1-quart saucepan. Stir in green onion and garlic. Bring to a boil over medium heat. Cook, uncovered, 5 minutes. Remove from heat. Stir in cilantro.

Sweet Pepper Pizza Fingers

2 tablespoons margarine or butter
2 large red, green and/or yellow bell peppers, thinly sliced
1 clove garlic, finely chopped
1 envelope LIPTON® RECIPE SECRETS® Onion Soup Mix
1 cup water
1 package (10 ounces) refrigerated pizza crust
1½ cups shredded mozzarella cheese (about 6 ounces), divided

Preheat oven to 425°F.

In 12-inch skillet, melt margarine over medium heat; cook peppers and garlic, stirring occasionally, 5 minutes or until peppers are tender. Stir in soup mix blended with water. Bring to a boil over high heat. Reduce heat to low and simmer, uncovered, 6 minutes or until liquid is absorbed. Remove from heat; set aside to cool 5 minutes.

Meanwhile, on baking sheet sprayed with nonstick cooking spray, roll out pizza crust into 12×8-inch rectangle. Sprinkle 1 cup mozzarella cheese over crust; top with cooked pepper mixture, spreading to edges of dough. Top with remaining ½ cup mozzarella cheese. Bake 10 minutes or until crust is golden brown and topping is bubbly. Remove from oven and let stand 5 minutes. To serve, cut into 4×1-inch strips. *Makes about 24 appetizers*

Serving Suggestion: Serve as a main dish by cutting pizza into Sicilian-style square pieces.

TIP **Purchase pre-cut pepper strips from the salad bar or produce section of the supermarket to reduce recipe preparation time. You'll have this delicious, colorful pizza in the oven in less than 15 minutes.**

Sweet Pepper Pizza Fingers

Glazed Meatballs

1 pound ground beef
½ cup fine dry breadcrumbs
⅓ cup minced onion
¼ cup milk
1 egg, beaten
1 tablespoon chopped parsley
1 teaspoon salt
½ teaspoon Worcestershire sauce
⅛ teaspoon pepper
2 tablespoons oil
1 cup (12-ounce jar) SMUCKER'S® Grape Jelly
½ cup bottled chili sauce

Combine ground beef, breadcrumbs, onion, milk, egg, parsley, salt, Worcestershire sauce and pepper; mix well. Shape into 1-inch meatballs. Cook in hot oil over medium heat for 10 to 15 minutes or until browned. Drain on paper towels.

Combine jelly and chili sauce in medium saucepan; stir well. Add meatballs; simmer 30 minutes, stirring occasionally. Serve in a chafing dish.

Makes about 5 dozen meatballs

Lit'l Party Delights

¾ cup chili sauce
¾ cup grape jelly
4 teaspoons red wine
2 teaspoons dry mustard
1½ teaspoons soy sauce
½ teaspoon ground ginger
½ teaspoon ground cinnamon
½ teaspoon ground nutmeg
1 pound HILLSHIRE FARM® Lit'l Smokies

Combine chili sauce, jelly, wine, mustard, soy sauce, ginger, cinnamon and nutmeg in medium saucepan; heat and stir over medium heat until mixture is smooth. Add Lit'l Smokies; heat 5 to 6 minutes or until hot. Serve with frilled toothpicks.

Makes about 50 hors d'oeuvres

Turkey Meatballs
with Sweet & Sour Sauce

1 pound ground turkey
½ cup seasoned bread crumbs
1 egg
1 tablespoon dried onion flakes
1 tablespoon green bell pepper, chopped
2 tablespoons hoisin sauce
½ cup lightly packed brown sugar
2 tablespoons cornstarch
1 can (20 ounces) pineapple chunks, drained
   and juice reserved
⅓ cup water
3 tablespoons rice wine vinegar
1 tablespoon reduced sodium soy sauce
1 large red bell pepper, cut into ½-inch cubes

Preheat oven to 400°F. In medium bowl, combine turkey, bread crumbs, egg, onion flakes, chopped green pepper and hoisin sauce. Mix well; cover and refrigerate for about 30 minutes or until mixture is well chilled. Shape 30 meatballs from turkey mixture (approximately 1 tablespoon for each meatball).

Coat 15×10×1-inch jelly-roll pan with nonstick cooking spray. Arrange meatballs on pan; bake 15 to 20 minutes or until meatballs are no longer pink in center.

Meanwhile, in 2-quart microwave-safe dish, combine brown sugar and cornstarch. Stir in reserved pineapple juice, water, vinegar and soy sauce. Microwave at HIGH (100% power) 2 minutes; stir in red pepper cubes. Microwave at HIGH 3 minutes, stirring halfway through cooking time. Fold in meatballs and pineapple chunks. Microwave at HIGH 2 minutes or until mixture is heated through. Transfer meatball mixture to chafing dish and serve with toothpicks.   *Makes 15 servings*

*Favorite recipe from **National Turkey Federation***

PARTY PICK-UPS

Mini Chickpea Cakes

- **1 can (15 ounces) chickpeas (garbanzo beans), rinsed and drained**
- **1 cup shredded carrots**
- **⅓ cup seasoned dry bread crumbs**
- **¼ cup creamy Italian salad dressing**
- **1 egg**

Preheat oven to 375°F. Spray baking sheet with nonstick cooking spray.

Mash chickpeas coarsely in medium bowl with hand potato masher. Stir in carrots, bread crumbs, salad dressing and egg; mix well.

Shape chickpea mixture into small patties, using about 1 tablespoon mixture for each. Place on prepared baking sheet.

Bake 15 to 18 minutes, turning halfway through baking time, until chickpea cakes are lightly browned on both sides. Serve warm with additional salad dressing for dipping, if desired.   *Makes about 2 dozen*

Mini Chickpea Cakes

Spinach-Artichoke Party Cups

36 small wonton wrappers (2½ to 3½ inches square)
 1 small can (8½ ounces) artichoke hearts, drained and
    chopped
 ½ package (10 ounces) frozen chopped spinach, thawed
    and well drained
 1 cup shredded Monterey Jack cheese
 ½ cup grated Parmesan cheese
 ½ cup mayonnaise
 1 clove garlic, minced

Preheat oven to 300°F. Spray mini muffin pan lightly with nonstick cooking spray. Press one wonton wrapper into each cup; spray lightly with cooking spray. Bake about 9 minutes or until light golden brown. Remove shells from muffin pan and set aside to cool. Repeat with remaining wonton wrappers.*

Meanwhile, combine artichoke hearts, spinach, cheeses, mayonnaise and garlic in medium bowl; mix well.

Fill wonton cups with spinach-artichoke mixture (about 1½ teaspoons). Place filled cups on baking sheet. Bake about 7 minutes or until heated through. Serve immediately.   *Makes 36 appetizers*

Wonton cups may be prepared up to one week in advance. Cool completely and store in an airtight container.

TIP
If you have leftover spinach-artichoke mixture after filling the wonton cups, bake in a shallow ovenproof dish at 350°F until hot and bubbly. Serve with bread or crackers.

Spinach-Artichoke Party Cups

Party Stuffed Pinwheels

1 envelope LIPTON® RECIPE SECRETS® Savory Herb with Garlic Soup Mix*
1 package (8 ounces) cream cheese, softened
1 cup shredded mozzarella cheese (about 4 ounces)
2 tablespoons milk
1 tablespoon grated Parmesan cheese
2 packages (10 ounces each) refrigerated pizza crust

*Also terrific with LIPTON® RECIPE SECRETS® Onion Soup Mix.

1. Preheat oven to 425°F. In medium bowl, combine all ingredients except pizza crusts; set aside.

2. Unroll pizza crusts, then top evenly with filling. Roll, starting at longest side, jelly-roll style. Cut into 32 rounds.**

3. On baking sheet sprayed with nonstick cooking spray, arrange rounds cut side down.

4. Bake, uncovered, 13 minutes or until golden brown.

Makes 32 pinwheels

**If rolled pizza crust is too soft to cut, refrigerate or freeze until firm.

TIP **To simplify last minute preparation, make the Pinwheel filling ahead of time and refrigerate. Bring the filling to room temperature before spreading over the crust.**

Party Stuffed Pinwheels

Chicken Empanadas

1 **box (15 ounces) refrigerated pie crusts (two 11-inch rounds)**
4 **ounces cream cheese**
2 **tablespoons chopped fresh cilantro**
2 **tablespoons salsa**
½ **teaspoon ground cumin**
½ **teaspoon salt**
¼ **teaspoon garlic powder**
1 **cup finely chopped cooked chicken**
1 **egg, beaten**
Additional salsa

Remove pie crust pouches from box; let stand at room temperature 15 to 20 minutes.

Heat cream cheese in small heavy saucepan over low heat; cook and stir until melted. Add cilantro, salsa, cumin, salt and garlic powder; stir until smooth. Stir in chicken; remove from heat.

Unfold pie crusts; remove plastic film. Roll out slightly on lightly floured surface. Cut crusts into 3-inch rounds using biscuit cutter or drinking glass. Reroll pie crust scraps and cut enough additional to equal 20 rounds.

Preheat oven to 425°F. Place about 2 teaspoons chicken mixture in center of each round. Brush edges lightly with water. Pull one side of dough over filling to form half circle; pinch edges to seal.

Place 10 to 12 empanadas on foil-lined baking sheet; brush lightly with egg. Bake 16 to 18 minutes or until lightly brown. Serve with salsa.

Makes 10 appetizer servings

TIP **Empanadas can be prepared ahead of time and frozen. Simply wrap unbaked empanadas with plastic wrap and freeze. Follow directions above and bake 18 to 20 minutes.**

Chicken Empanadas

Sausage-Bacon-Apricot Kabobs

**1 package BOB EVANS® Italian Grillin' Sausage
(approximately 5 links)**
1 cup dried apricot halves
8 slices bacon
3 tablespoons apricot preserves
3 tablespoons lemon juice
1 tablespoon Dijon mustard
1 teaspoon Worcestershire sauce

Precook sausage 10 minutes in gently boiling water. Drain and cut into ¾-inch slices. Alternate sausage and apricots on 8 wooden skewers,* weaving bacon back and forth in ribbonlike fashion between them. Grill or broil over medium-high heat 3 to 4 minutes on each side. Combine preserves, lemon juice, mustard and Worcestershire in small bowl. Brush preserves mixture on kabobs; continue grilling, turning and basting frequently, until bacon is cooked through. Refrigerate leftovers.   *Makes 8 kabobs*

*Soak wooden skewers in water 30 minutes before using to prevent burning.

Smoked Ham & Roasted Red Pepper Roll-Ups

⅔ cup cream cheese, softened
½ cup shredded mozzarella or Cheddar cheese
½ cup chopped roasted red peppers, drained
¼ cup *French's*® Bold n' Spicy Brown Mustard
6 (10-inch) flour tortillas
¾ pound thinly sliced smoked ham

1. Beat cream cheese, mozzarella cheese, red peppers and mustard in medium bowl until smooth. Spread about ¼ *cup* mixture evenly on each tortilla.

2. Arrange ham on top. Roll up tortillas jelly-roll style. Cut into 2-inch pieces.
Makes 12 servings

Prep Time: 15 minutes

Sausage-Bacon-Apricot Kabobs

Spinach-Stuffed Appetizer Shells

18 jumbo pasta shells (about 6 ounces)
1 package (10 ounces) frozen chopped spinach, thawed and well drained
1 can (8 ounces) water chestnuts, drained and chopped
¾ cup fat-free ricotta cheese
½ cup reduced-fat mayonnaise
¼ cup finely chopped carrot
3 tablespoons finely chopped onion
¾ teaspoon garlic powder
¾ teaspoon hot pepper sauce

1. Cook shells according to package directions, omitting salt. Rinse under cold running water until shells are cool; drain well.

2. Combine remaining ingredients in medium bowl; mix well.

3. Fill each shell with about 3 tablespoons spinach mixture; cover. Refrigerate up to 12 hours before serving. Garnish, if desired.   *Makes 18 shells*

Southwestern Roll-Ups

2 packages (8 ounces each) cream cheese, softened
¾ cup prepared salsa
1 envelope LIPTON® RECIPE SECRETS® Onion Soup Mix
1 package (14 ounces) flour tortillas
1 medium head green leaf lettuce (about 16 leaves)

1. In large bowl, with electric mixer, beat cream cheese until light and fluffy, about 2 minutes. Stir in salsa and soup mix. Spread ⅓ cup cheese mixture on one tortilla, leaving ½ inch edge. Top with 2 lettuce leaves. Roll up tortilla and wrap tightly in plastic wrap.

2. Repeat with remaining ingredients for each tortilla. Refrigerate until cheese mixture has set, about 1 hour.

3. To serve, slice each roll 1 inch thick on the diagonal. Secure with fancy toothpicks.   *Makes about 50 servings*

Prep Time: 10 minutes
Chill Time: 1 hour

Spinach-Stuffed Appetizer Shells

Onion and Pepper Calzones

1 teaspoon vegetable oil
½ cup chopped onion
½ cup chopped green bell pepper
¼ teaspoon salt
⅛ teaspoon dried basil leaves
⅛ teaspoon dried oregano leaves
⅛ teaspoon black pepper
1 can (12 ounces) country biscuits (10 biscuits)
¼ cup (1 ounce) shredded mozzarella cheese
½ cup prepared spaghetti or pizza sauce
2 tablespoons grated Parmesan cheese

1. Preheat oven to 400°F. Heat oil in medium nonstick skillet over medium-high heat. Add onion and bell pepper. Cook 5 minutes, stirring occasionally. Remove from heat. Add salt, basil, oregano and black pepper; stir to combine. Cool slightly.

2. While onion mixture is cooling, flatten biscuits into 3½-inch circles about ⅛-inch thick using palm of hand.

3. Stir mozzarella cheese into onion mixture; spoon 1 teaspoonful onto each biscuit. Fold biscuits in half, covering filling. Press edges with tines of fork to seal; transfer to baking sheet.

4. Bake 10 to 12 minutes or until golden brown. While calzones are baking, place spaghetti sauce in small microwavable bowl. Cover with vented plastic wrap. Microwave at HIGH 3 minutes or until hot.

5. To serve, spoon spaghetti sauce and Parmesan cheese evenly over each calzone. Serve immediately. *Makes 10 appetizers*

Prep and Cook Time: 25 minutes

Onion and Pepper Calzones

Thai Satay Chicken Skewers

1 **pound boneless skinless chicken breasts**
⅓ **cup soy sauce**
2 **tablespoons fresh lime juice**
2 **cloves garlic, minced**
1 **teaspoon grated fresh ginger**
¾ **teaspoon red pepper flakes**
2 **tablespoons water**
¾ **cup canned unsweetened coconut milk**
1 **tablespoon creamy peanut butter**
4 **green onions with tops, cut into 1-inch pieces**

1. Slice chicken crosswise into ⅜-inch-wide strips; place in shallow glass dish.

2. Combine soy sauce, lime juice, garlic, ginger and red pepper flakes in small bowl. Reserve 3 tablespoons mixture; cover and refrigerate until preparing peanut sauce. Add water to remaining mixture. Pour over chicken; toss to coat well. Cover; marinate in refrigerator at least 30 minutes or up to 2 hours, stirring mixture occasionally.

3. Soak 16 (5- to 6-inch) wooden skewers in water 20 minutes before using to prevent them from burning. Prepare grill for direct cooking.

4. Meanwhile, for peanut sauce, combine coconut milk, reserved soy sauce mixture and peanut butter in small saucepan. Bring to a boil over medium-high heat, stirring constantly. Reduce heat to low and simmer, uncovered, 2 to 4 minutes or until sauce thickens. Keep warm.

5. Drain chicken; reserve marinade from dish. Weave 3 to 4 chicken pieces accordion style onto each skewer, alternating with green onion pieces placed crosswise on skewer. Brush reserved marinade from dish over chicken and onions. Discard remaining marinade.

6. Place skewers on grid. Grill skewers on uncovered grill over medium-hot coals 6 to 8 minutes or until chicken is no longer pink in center, turning halfway through grilling time. Serve with warm peanut sauce for dipping.

Makes 16 appetizer servings

Thai Satay Chicken Skewers

Festive Taco Cups

1 tablespoon vegetable oil
½ cup chopped onion
½ pound ground turkey or ground beef
1 clove garlic, minced
½ teaspoon dried oregano leaves
½ teaspoon chili powder or taco seasoning
¼ teaspoon salt
1¼ cups shredded taco-flavored cheese or Mexican cheese blend, divided
1 can (11½ ounces) refrigerated corn breadstick dough
Chopped fresh tomato and sliced green onion for garnish (optional)

Heat oil in large skillet over medium heat. Add onion and cook until tender. Add turkey; cook until turkey is no longer pink, stirring occasionally. Stir in garlic, oregano, chili powder and salt. Remove from heat and stir in ½ cup cheese; set aside.

Preheat oven to 375°F. Lightly grease 36 miniature (1¾-inch) muffin pan cups. Remove dough from container but do not unroll dough. Separate dough into 8 pieces at perforations. Divide each piece into 3 pieces; roll or pat each piece into 3-inch circle. Press circles into prepared muffin pan cups.

Fill each cup with 1½ to 2 teaspoons turkey mixture. Bake 10 minutes. Sprinkle tops of taco cups with remaining ¾ cup cheese; bake 2 to 3 minutes more until cheese is melted. Garnish with tomato and green onion, if desired.

Makes 36 taco cups

Festive Taco Cups

Cheddar Chili Tomato Pots

  6 medium tomatoes
3½ cups (14 ounces) Sargento® Fancy Sharp Cheddar Shredded
    Cheese, divided
  2 cans (4 ounces each) diced green chiles, well drained
  ½ teaspoon dried oregano leaves, crushed
  ½ teaspoon minced garlic
  6 tablespoons sour cream
  3 green onions, sliced
    Breadsticks for serving

1. Preheat oven to 325°F. Grease 11×7-inch baking dish. Cut ½-inch slice from top of each tomato; scoop out pulp and seeds, leaving ¼-inch shell (save pulp for another use such as salads or sauces).

2. Invert tomatoes on paper towel-lined plate; let drain 20 minutes.

3. Combine 3 cups cheese, chiles, oregano and garlic in medium bowl.

4. Using large spoon, stuff tomato shells with cheese mixture.

5. Arrange tomato shells in prepared dish. Bake 20 minutes. Top with sour cream, remaining ½ cup cheese and green onions. Serve with breadsticks.

Makes 6 first-course servings

TIP **To make this recipe for a colorful party sampler tray, use cherry or small tomatoes. Scoop out the pulp with a melon ball utensil. Stuff and bake just until cheese is melted. Your guests will devour these flavorful bites.**

Cheddar Chili Tomato Pots

Dried Tomato Party Pockets

¼ cup SONOMA Dried Tomato Bits*
2 tablespoons boiling water
1 cup (4 ounces) shredded sharp Cheddar cheese
3 tablespoons sliced green onions
1 package (10 ounces) prepared refrigerated biscuits
   (10 biscuits)
1 egg, beaten
2 teaspoons sesame seeds (optional)

*To substitute dried tomato halves for tomato bits, measure ½ cup SONOMA Dried Tomato halves into blender; pulse using on/off button until finely chopped.

Preheat oven to 400°F. Mix tomato bits and water in medium bowl; set aside 5 minutes. Add cheese and onions; toss to blend evenly. Roll out each biscuit to 4- to 5-inch circle on lightly floured surface. For each pocket, place about 2 tablespoons tomato mixture onto center of circle. Brush edge with egg. Fold over and press to seal completely. Place, 2 inches apart, on baking sheet. Brush with egg and sprinkle with sesame seeds, if desired. Bake 10 to 12 minutes or until golden brown. Serve warm or at room temperature.

Makes 10 (4-inch) pockets

TIP Fix party pockets for half-time snacks or spur-of-the-moment parties. They are best served freshly baked. The pockets can also be frozen after baking. To serve, thaw and reheat in the oven until warm and crispy.

Dried Tomato Party Pockets

Mushrooms Rockefeller

18 large fresh button mushrooms (about 1 pound)
2 slices bacon
¼ cup chopped onion
1 package (10 ounces) frozen chopped spinach, thawed and squeezed dry
1 tablespoon lemon juice
1 teaspoon grated lemon peel
½ jar (2 ounces) chopped pimiento, drained
Lemon slices and lemon balm for garnish

1. Lightly spray 13×9-inch baking dish with nonstick cooking spray. Preheat oven to 375°F. Brush dirt from mushrooms; clean by wiping mushrooms with damp paper towel. Pull entire stem out of each mushroom cap.

2. Cut thin slice from base of each stem; discard. Chop stems.

3. Cook bacon in medium skillet over medium heat until crisp. Remove bacon with tongs to paper towel; set aside. Add mushroom stems and onion to hot drippings in skillet. Cook and stir until onion is soft. Add spinach, lemon juice, lemon peel and pimiento; blend well. Stuff mushroom caps with spinach mixture; place in single layer in prepared baking dish. Crumble reserved bacon and sprinkle on top of mushrooms. Bake 15 minutes or until heated through. Garnish, if desired. Serve immediately.

Makes 18 appetizers

Mushrooms Rockefeller

Tortellini Kabobs

2 tablespoons olive oil
1 large clove garlic, minced
1 can (15 ounces) CONTADINA® Tomato Sauce
2 tablespoons rinsed capers
2 tablespoons chopped fresh basil leaves
1 teaspoon Italian herb seasoning
¼ teaspoon red pepper flakes
6 cups of the following kabob ingredients: cooked, drained
     meat- or cheese-filled tortellini, cocktail franks, cooked
     shrimp, whole button mushrooms, bell pepper chunks,
     cooked broccoli, cooked cauliflowerets, onion pieces

1. Heat oil in medium saucepan over medium-high heat. Add garlic; cook and stir until lightly browned. Stir in tomato sauce, capers, basil, Italian seasoning and red pepper flakes.

2. Bring to a boil. Reduce heat to low; simmer 5 to 10 minutes, stirring occasionally.

3. Combine kabob ingredients in medium bowl; cover with tomato sauce mixture.

4. Marinate in refrigerator 15 minutes or longer, if desired, stirring occasionally. Place on skewers.

5. Broil 5 inches from heat source until heated through, turning once during cooking and brushing with any remaining tomato sauce mixture.

Makes 12 appetizer servings

Prep Time: 15 minutes
Marinate Time: 15 minutes
Cook Time: 15 minutes

Tortellini Kabobs

Antipasto Crescent Bites

2 ounces cream cheese (do not use reduced-fat or fat-free cream cheese)
1 package (8 ounces) refrigerated crescent roll dough
1 egg plus 1 tablespoon water, beaten
4 strips roasted red pepper, cut into 3×¾-inch-long strips
2 large marinated artichoke hearts, cut in half lengthwise to ¾-inch width
1 thin slice Genoa or other salami, cut into 4 strips
4 small stuffed green olives, cut into halves

1. Preheat oven to 375°F. Cut cream cheese into 16 equal pieces, about 1 teaspoon per piece; set aside. Remove dough from package. Unroll on lightly floured surface. Cut each triangle of dough in half to form 2 triangles. Brush outer edges of triangle lightly with egg mixture.

2. Wrap 1 pepper strip around 1 piece of cream cheese. Place on dough triangle. Fold over and pinch edges to seal; repeat with remaining pepper strips. Place 1 piece artichoke heart and 1 piece of cream cheese on dough triangle. Fold over and pinch edges to seal; repeat with remaining pieces of artichoke hearts. Wrap 1 strip salami around 1 piece of cream cheese. Place on dough triangle. Fold over and pinch edges to seal; repeat with remaining salami. Place 2 olive halves and 1 piece of cream cheese on dough triangle. Fold over and pinch edges to seal; repeat with remaining olives. Place on ungreased baking sheet. Brush with egg mixture.

3. Bake 12 to 14 minutes or until golden brown. Cool on wire rack. Store in airtight container in refrigerator.

4. Reheat on baking sheet in preheated 325°F oven 7 to 8 minutes or until warmed through. Do not microwave. *Makes 16 pieces*

Antipasto Crescent Bites

Taco Stuffed Mushrooms

1 pound medium-sized fresh white mushrooms
3 tablespoons vegetable oil, divided
½ cup sliced green onions
½ cup crushed nacho-flavored tortilla chips
Pinch ground red pepper
½ cup shredded hot-pepper Jack cheese
½ cup sliced cherry tomatoes

Preheat oven to 450°F. Remove stems from mushrooms. Place caps, stem-side-up, in shallow baking pan. Brush outside surface lightly with 2 tablespoons vegetable oil; set aside. Chop mushroom stems. Heat remaining 1 tablespoon vegetable oil in medium skillet until hot; add mushroom stems. Cook about 2 minutes, stirring frequently until softened. Add green onions, tortilla chips and red pepper. Cook about 2 minutes, stirring constantly until onions are tender. Remove from heat; cool slightly. Stir in cheese. Fill reserved mushroom caps with onion mixture; top each with 1 tomato slice. Bake about 10 minutes or until mushrooms are tender and hot. Serve hot or warm.

Makes about 2 dozen mushrooms

*Favorite recipe from **Mushroom Council***

TIP Since mushrooms absorb moisture, do not wash mushrooms until you are ready to use them. The best way to wash mushrooms is to wipe them clean with a damp paper towel instead of soaking them in water.

Left to right: Taco Stuffed Mushrooms, Roasted
Red Pepper Stuffed Mushrooms (page 158)

French-Style Pizza Bites
(Pissaladière)

2 tablespoons olive oil
1 medium onion, thinly sliced
1 medium red bell pepper, cut into strips
2 cloves garlic, minced
⅓ cup pitted black olives, each cut into thin wedges
1 can (10 ounces) refrigerated pizza crust dough
¾ cup (3 ounces) finely shredded Swiss or Gruyère cheese

1. Position oven rack to lowest position. Preheat oven to 425°F. Grease large baking sheet.

2. Heat oil until hot in medium skillet over medium heat. Add onion, pepper and garlic. Cook and stir 5 minutes or until vegetables are crisp-tender. Stir in olives; remove from heat.

3. Pat dough into 16×12-inch rectangle on prepared baking sheet.

4. Arrange vegetables over dough; sprinkle with cheese. Bake 10 minutes. Loosen crust from baking sheet; slide crust onto oven rack. Bake 3 to 5 minutes or until golden brown.

5. Slide baking sheet back under crust to remove crust from rack. Transfer to cutting board. Cut dough crosswise into eight 1¾-inch-wide strips. Cut dough diagonally into ten 2-inch-wide strips, making diamond pieces. Serve immediately. *Makes about 24 servings (2 diamonds per serving)*

French-Style Pizza Bites (Pissaladière)

Quick Sausage Appetizers

½ pound **BOB EVANS® Italian Roll Sausage**
⅓ **cup mozzarella cheese**
¼ **cup sour cream**
3 **tablespoons mayonnaise**
2 **tablespoons chopped green onion**
½ **teaspoon Worcestershire sauce**
10 **slices white bread***

Party rye or thinly sliced French bread can be used instead of white bread. Double recipe to have enough sausage mixture.

Preheat broiler. Crumble and cook sausage in medium skillet until browned. Drain on paper towels. Transfer sausage to small bowl; stir in cheese, sour cream, mayonnaise, green onion and Worcestershire. Cut crusts from bread. Cut each slice into 4 squares; spread about 1 teaspoon sausage mixture onto each square. Arrange squares on ungreased baking sheet; place under hot broiler just until cheese melts and topping bubbles. (Be careful not to burn corners and edges.) Serve hot.   *Makes 40 appetizer squares*

> **TIP** Quick Sausage Appetizers may be made ahead and refrigerated overnight or frozen up to 1 month before broiling.

Quick Sausage Appetizers

Spinach Feta Triangles

¼ **cup olive oil**
½ **cup chopped onion**
2 **eggs**
3 **packages (10 ounces each) frozen chopped spinach, thawed and well drained**
16 **ounces feta cheese, drained and crumbled**
½ **cup minced fresh parsley**
2 **tablespoons chopped fresh oregano leaves** *or* **1 teaspoon dried oregano leaves**
  Salt and black pepper to taste
1 **package (16 ounces) frozen phyllo dough, thawed to room temperature**
2 **cups butter, melted**

1. Preheat oven to 375°F. Heat oil over medium-high heat in small skillet. Add onion; cook and stir until translucent and golden.

2. Beat eggs in large bowl with an electric mixer on medium-high speed until light and lemon colored. Add onion mixture, spinach, feta cheese, parsley and oregano; stir until blended. Season with salt and pepper.

3. Remove phyllo from package; unroll and place on large sheet of waxed paper. Fold phyllo crosswise into thirds. Use scissors to cut along folds into thirds. Cover phyllo with large sheet of plastic wrap and damp, clean kitchen towel. Phyllo dries out quickly if not covered.

4. Lay 1 strip of phyllo at a time on flat surface and brush immediately with melted butter. Fold strip in half lengthwise. Brush with butter again. Place rounded teaspoonful of spinach filling on 1 end of strip; fold over 1 corner to make triangle. Continue folding end to end, as you would fold a flag, keeping edges straight. Brush top with butter. Repeat process until all filling is used up.

5. Place triangles in single layer, seam side down, on ungreased baking sheet. Bake 20 minutes or until lightly browned. Serve warm.

Makes 5 dozen appetizers

Spinach Feta Triangles

FESTIVE FLAIR

Spinach Cheese Bundles

**1 container (6½ ounces) garlic- and herb-flavored
   spreadable cheese**
½ cup chopped fresh spinach
¼ teaspoon pepper
**1 package (17¼ ounces) frozen puff pastry, thawed
   Sweet and sour or favorite dipping sauce (optional)**

Preheat oven to 400°F. Combine spreadable cheese, spinach and pepper in small bowl; mix well.

Roll out one sheet puff pastry dough on floured surface into 12-inch square. Cut into 16 (3-inch) individual squares. Place about 1 teaspoon cheese mixture in center of each square; brush edges of squares with water. Bring edges together up over filling and twist tightly to seal; fan out corners of puff pastry.

Place bundles 2 inches apart on baking sheet. Bake about 13 minutes or until golden brown. Repeat with remaining sheet of puff pastry and cheese mixture. Serve warm with dipping sauce, if desired.

Makes 32 bundles

Spinach Cheese Bundles

Pesto Cheesecake

CRUST
- **1 cup fine dry bread crumbs**
- **½ cup very finely chopped toasted pine nuts or walnuts**
- **3 tablespoons melted butter or margarine**

FILLING
- **2 cups (15 ounces) SARGENTO® Light Ricotta Cheese**
- **½ cup half-and-half**
- **2 tablespoons all-purpose flour**
- **½ teaspoon salt**
- **2 eggs**
- **⅓ cup Homemade Pesto Sauce (recipe follows) or prepared pesto sauce**

Preheat oven to 350°F. Lightly grease sides of 8- or 9-inch springform pan.

Combine bread crumbs, nuts and butter in small bowl until well blended. Press evenly onto bottom of pan. Refrigerate until ready to use.

Combine Ricotta cheese, half-and-half, flour and salt in medium bowl with electric mixer. Beat at medium speed until smooth. Add eggs, one at a time; beat until smooth. Pour into prepared crust. Spoon pesto by teaspoonsful randomly over cheese mixture. Gently swirl with knife for marbled effect.

Bake 45 minutes or until center is just set; turn off oven. Cool in oven with door open 30 minutes. Remove from oven. Cool completely on wire rack. Cut into thin slices before serving. *Makes 10 servings*

Homemade Pesto Sauce: In food processor or blender, mince 1 clove garlic. Add ½ cup packed fresh basil leaves and 1 tablespoon toasted pine nuts or walnuts. Process until smooth, scraping down side of bowl once. With machine running, drizzle 2 tablespoons olive oil into bowl; process until smooth. Add ¼ cup (1 ounce) SARGENTO® Fancy Parmesan Shredded Cheese; process just until cheese is blended.

Pesto Cheesecake

Santa Fe Shrimp Martini Cocktails

1 jar (16 ounces) mild salsa
1 ripe small avocado, peeled and chopped
1 tablespoon *Frank's® RedHot® Cayenne Pepper Sauce*
1 tablespoon lime juice
1 tablespoon chopped fresh cilantro leaves
1 pound large shrimp, cooked, peeled and deveined
1 cup *French's® French Fried Onions*
1 lime, cut into 6 wedges

1. Combine salsa, avocado, *Frank's® RedHot* Sauce, lime juice and cilantro in large bowl. Alternately layer shrimp and salsa mixture in 6 margarita or martini glasses.

2. Microwave French Fried Onions on HIGH for 1 minute until golden. Sprinkle over shrimp. Garnish with lime wedges.   *Makes 6 servings*

Note: Purchase cooked, cleaned shrimp from the seafood section of your local supermarket.

Prep Time: 10 minutes
Cook Time: 1 minute

TIP **Shrimp may be peeled and deveined either before or after they are cooked. To remove the peel, start on the side with the legs and lift the peel up and over, then back around to the leg side. To devein, make a small cut along the back and lift out the dark vein with the tip of a knife.**

Santa Fe Shrimp Martini Cocktail and Crab
Cakes with Horseradish Mustard Sauce (page 171)

153

Pepper Cheese Cocktail Puffs

½ package (17¼ ounces) frozen puff pastry, thawed
1 tablespoon Dijon mustard
½ cup (2 ounces) finely shredded Cheddar cheese
1 teaspoon cracked black pepper
1 egg
1 tablespoon water

1. Preheat oven to 400°F. Grease baking sheets.

2. Roll out 1 sheet puff pastry dough on well floured surface to 14×10-inch rectangle. Spread half of dough (from 10-inch side) with mustard. Sprinkle with cheese and pepper. Fold dough over filling; roll gently to seal edges.

3. Cut lengthwise into 3 strips; cut each strip diagonally into 1½-inch pieces. Place on prepared baking sheets. Beat egg and water in small bowl; brush on appetizers.

4. Bake appetizers 12 to 15 minutes or until puffed and deep golden brown. Remove from baking sheet to wire rack to cool.

Makes about 20 appetizers

Prep and Bake Time: 30 minutes

TIP For the best puffs, work quickly and efficiently with the puff pastry. The colder puff pastry is, the better it will puff in the hot oven. Double this recipe for tasty bites that will be gone before the oven is cool.

Pepper Cheese Cocktail Puffs

Cranberry-Walnut Pear Wedges

3 firm ripe pears, cut into quarters and cored
¼ cup triple sec*
2 tablespoons orange juice
½ cup prepared cranberry fruit relish
¼ cup finely chopped walnuts
¼ cup (1 ounce) crumbled blue cheese

*Omit liqueur, if desired. Increase orange juice to ¼ cup. Add 2 tablespoons honey and 2 tablespoons balsamic vinegar to marinade.

1. Place pears in resealable plastic food storage bag. Pour liqueur and orange juice over pears; seal bag. Turn bag over several times to coat pears evenly. Refrigerate at least 1 hour, turning bag occasionally.

2. Drain pears; discard marinade. Place pears on serving platter. Spoon cranberry relish evenly into cavities of pears; sprinkle with walnuts and cheese. Garnish, if desired.   *Makes 12 servings*

Brie Torte

1 (15- to 16-ounce) wheel Brie cheese
6 tablespoons butter, softened
⅓ cup chopped dried tart cherries
¼ cup finely chopped pecans
½ teaspoon dried thyme *or* 2 teaspoons
    finely chopped fresh thyme

Refrigerate Brie until chilled and firm or freeze 30 minutes until firm. Cut Brie in half horizontally.

Combine butter, cherries, pecans and thyme in small bowl; mix well. Spread mixture evenly onto cut side of one half of Brie. Top with other half, cut side down. Lightly press together. Wrap in plastic wrap; refrigerate 1 to 2 hours. To serve, cut into serving size wedges and bring to room temperature. Serve with water crackers.   *Makes about 20 appetizer servings*

Note: If wrapped securely in plastic wrap, this appetizer will keep in the refrigerator for at least a week.

*Favorite recipe from **Cherry Marketing Institute***

Cranberry-Walnut Pear Wedge

Shrimp and Snow Pea Appetizers with Currant Mustard Sauce

6 ounces fresh snow peas (about 36)
1½ pounds medium shrimp, cooked and peeled

CURRANT MUSTARD SAUCE
¾ cup SMUCKER'S® Currant Jelly
¼ cup Dijon mustard

Blanch snow peas in boiling salted water for 45 seconds. Immediately drain and run under cold water.

Wrap 1 blanched pea pod around each shrimp and secure with toothpick.

Combine jelly and mustard; beat with a fork or wire whisk until smooth. (Jelly will dissolve in about 5 minutes.) Serve sauce with appetizers.

Makes 36 appetizers

Roasted Red Pepper Stuffed Mushrooms

1 pound medium-sized fresh white mushrooms
1 package (8 ounces) cream cheese, softened
¼ cup roasted red peppers, patted dry
2 tablespoons grated Parmesan cheese
1 teaspoon minced garlic
Pinch ground red pepper
Toasted pine nuts, sliced green olives and
parsley leaves, for garnish (optional)

Remove stems from mushrooms; reserve caps. Set stems aside for another use. Place cream cheese, roasted red peppers, Parmesan cheese, garlic and ground red pepper in food processor fitted with metal blade; process until smooth. Place cream cheese mixture in pastry bag fitted with large star tip. Pipe into mushroom caps; garnish with pine nuts, green olives and parsley leaves, if desired.

Makes about 2 dozen mushrooms

Favorite recipe from **Mushroom Council**

Shrimp and Snow Pea Appetizers
with Currant Mustard Sauce

Ham Spirals

1 (3-ounce) package cream cheese, softened
¼ cup finely chopped dried tart cherries
3 tablespoons finely chopped pecans
2 tablespoons mayonnaise
½ teaspoon honey mustard or spicy brown mustard
4 thin slices cooked ham

Combine cream cheese, dried cherries, pecans, mayonnaise and mustard in small bowl; mix well.

Spread cherry mixture evenly on ham slices. Roll up jelly-roll style; fasten with wooden picks. Let chill several hours. Remove wooden picks. Slice each ham roll crosswise into ¼-inch slices; serve with crackers.

Makes about 40 (¼-inch) pieces

Favorite recipe from **Cherry Marketing Institute**

Crème de Brie Phyllo Tartlets with Caramelized Onion

1 tablespoon butter
1 large sweet onion (preferably Vidalia), diced
2 teaspoons sugar
1 (2.1-ounce) box frozen prebaked phyllo tartlet shells
1 (5-ounce) package ALOUETTE® Crème de Brie®, any variety
2 tablespoons fresh chopped parsley

Preheat oven to 375°F. Melt butter in small skillet over medium heat. Add onion and sauté until golden. Just when onion begins to brown, sprinkle with sugar and continue cooking until golden brown. Fill each phyllo shell with heaping teaspoon Crème de Brie and top with ½ teaspoon caramelized onion. Place on baking sheet; warm in oven about 5 minutes. Garnish with parsley and serve immediately.

Makes 15 appetizers

Arugula-Prosciutto
Wrapped Breadsticks
with Garlic Mustard Sauce

- ½ **cup mayonnaise**
- 6 **tablespoons grated Parmesan cheese**
- 2 **tablespoons** *French's*® **Napa Valley style Dijon Mustard**
- 1 **tablespoon chopped fresh basil**
- 2 **teaspoons minced garlic**
- 1 **package (4½ ounces) long breadsticks (12 to 16 breadsticks)**
- 1⅓ **cups** *French's*® **French Fried Onions, crushed**
- ½ **pound thinly sliced prosciutto or smoked deli ham**
- 1 **bunch arugula (about 20 leaves) or green leaf lettuce, washed, drained and stems removed**

1. Combine mayonnaise, cheese, mustard, basil and garlic in mixing bowl. Spread half of each breadstick with some of mustard sauce. Roll in French Fried Onions, pressing firmly.

2. Arrange prosciutto slices on flat work surface. Top each slice with leaf of arugula. Place coated end of breadsticks on top; roll up jelly-roll style. Place seam side down on serving platter.

3. Serve wrapped breadsticks with remaining mustard sauce for dipping.

Makes 16 appetizers

Prep Time: 25 minutes

Elegant Pork Terrine

2 tablespoons butter or margarine
1 cup chopped onion
2 cloves garlic, minced
1 pound sweet Italian sausage
1 pound ground pork
2 eggs, slightly beaten
¼ cup light cream
2 tablespoons brandy
⅛ teaspoon ground allspice
⅛ teaspoon ground cloves
⅛ teaspoon black pepper
½ pound Canadian bacon, cut into 4×½-inch strips
8 fresh asparagus spears

In large skillet melt butter. Add onion and garlic; cook and stir until tender. Remove from skillet and set aside.

Remove sausage from casing and crumble into skillet. Add ground pork and cook 4 minutes or until partially cooked. Drain pan drippings. Let pork mixture stand about 10 minutes to cool. Stir in onion mixture, eggs, light cream, brandy, allspice, cloves and pepper; mix well.

Spread ⅓ of meat mixture in lightly greased 8×4×2-inch loaf pan. Place Canadian-style bacon, end to end, over meat mixture, making 3 rows. Top with ⅓ of meat mixture. Remove tough ends of asparagus. Peel lower stalks to remove scales. Place asparagus, end to end, over meat mixture, making 4 rows. Top with remaining ⅓ of meat mixture.

Wrap entire loaf pan with heavy-duty foil, sealing edges. Fill large roasting pan about half full of water. Place loaf pan in roasting pan. Bake at 350°F 1 to 1½ hours or until done. Remove loaf pan from roasting pan; let stand about 15 minutes. Place another loaf pan filled with dried beans on top of terrine. Let stand 2 hours. Remove weight and refrigerate terrine overnight.

To serve, remove foil and loosen edges of terrine with knife. Turn out onto serving platter. Serve with assorted crackers. *Makes 16 servings*

Prep Time: 30 minutes
Cook Time: 90 minutes

*Favorite recipe from **National Pork Board***

Elegant Pork Terrine

Pastry Puffs
with Goat Cheese and Spinach

1 (12-ounce) package BOB EVANS® Original Links
30 to 40 leaves fresh spinach
**1 (17¾-ounce) package frozen puff pastry sheets, thawed
    according to package directions**
⅓ cup goat cheese*
3 tablespoons Dijon mustard

*For a milder flavor, substitute plain or herb cream cheese for goat cheese.

Cook sausage in large skillet until browned. Drain on paper towels; let cool.
Steam spinach; let cool. Preheat oven to 375°F. Cut 1 pastry sheet evenly into
9 squares. Cut 5 additional squares from second sheet (remaining pastry may
be refrozen for future use). Stretch or roll squares slightly to form rectangles.
Line each rectangle with 2 or 3 spinach leaves, leaving ¼ inch on 1 short end
to seal edges. Spread about 1 teaspoon goat cheese over spinach; spread
½ teaspoon mustard over goat cheese. Arrange sausage across short end and
roll up pastry and filling, pressing to seal edges. Place on *ungreased* baking
sheet, seam sides down. Bake 14 to 16 minutes or until golden. Cut each puff
into halves or thirds. Refrigerate leftovers.   *Makes 28 to 42 appetizers*

> ## TIP   Pastry puffs may be made ahead
> **and refrigerated overnight or frozen up to
> 1 month. Reheat in oven when ready to serve.**

Pastry Puffs with Goat Cheese and Spinach

Jicama & Shrimp Cocktail with Roasted Red Pepper Sauce

2 large red bell peppers
6 ounces (about 24 medium-large) shrimp, peeled and deveined
1 medium clove garlic
1½ cups fresh cilantro sprigs
2 tablespoons lime juice
2 tablespoons orange juice
½ teaspoon hot pepper sauce
1 small jicama (about ¾ pound), peeled and cut into strips
1 plum tomato, halved, seeded and thinly sliced

1. Place bell peppers on broiler pan. Broil, 4 to 6 inches from heat, about 6 minutes, turning every 2 to 3 minutes or until all sides are charred. Transfer peppers to paper bag; close bag tightly. Let stand 10 minutes or until peppers are cool enough to handle and skins are loosened. Peel peppers; cut in half. Remove cores, seeds and membranes; discard.

2. Add shrimp to large saucepan of boiling water. Reduce heat to medium-low; simmer, uncovered, 2 to 3 minutes or until shrimp turn pink. Drain shrimp; rinse under cold running water. Cover; refrigerate until ready to use.

3. Place peppers and garlic in food processor; process until peppers are coarsely chopped. Add cilantro, lime juice, orange juice and pepper sauce; process until cilantro is finely chopped but mixture is not puréed.

4. Combine jicama, shrimp and tomato in large bowl. Add bell pepper mixture; toss to coat evenly. Serve over lettuce. *Makes 8 servings*

Herbed Blue Cheese Spread with Garlic Toasts

1⅓ cups low-fat (1%) cottage cheese
1¼ cups (5 ounces) crumbled blue, feta or goat cheese
1 large clove garlic
2 teaspoons lemon juice
2 green onions with tops, sliced (about ¼ cup)
¼ cup chopped fresh basil or oregano *or* 1 teaspoon
dried basil or oregano leaves
2 tablespoons toasted slivered almonds*
Garlic Toasts (recipe follows)

*To toast almonds, place almonds in shallow baking pan. Bake in preheated 350°F oven 8 to 10 minutes or until lightly toasted, stirring occasionally.

1. Combine cottage cheese, blue cheese, garlic and lemon juice in food processor; process until smooth. Add green onions, basil and almonds; pulse until well blended but still chunky.

2. Spoon cheese spread into small serving bowl; cover. Refrigerate until ready to serve.

3. When ready to serve, prepare Garlic Toasts. Spread 1 tablespoon cheese spread onto each toast slice. Garnish, if desired. *Makes 16 servings*

Garlic Toasts

32 French bread slices, ½ inch thick
Nonstick cooking spray
¼ teaspoon garlic powder
⅛ teaspoon salt

Place bread slices on nonstick baking sheet. Lightly coat both sides of bread slices with nonstick cooking spray. Combine garlic powder and salt in small bowl; sprinkle evenly onto bread slices. Broil, 6 to 8 inches from heat, 30 to 45 seconds on each side or until bread slices are lightly toasted on both sides.

Makes 32 pieces

Herbed Blue Cheese Spread with Garlic Toasts

Tuscan White Bean Crostini

2 cans (15 ounces each) white beans (such as Great Northern
    or cannellini), rinsed and drained
½ large red bell pepper, finely chopped *or* ⅓ cup finely
    chopped roasted red bell pepper
⅓ cup finely chopped onion
⅓ cup red wine vinegar
3 tablespoons chopped fresh parsley
1 tablespoon olive oil
2 cloves garlic, minced
½ teaspoon dried oregano leaves
¼ teaspoon black pepper
18 French bread slices, about ¼ inch thick

1. Combine beans, bell pepper and onion in large bowl.

2. Whisk together vinegar, parsley, oil, garlic, oregano and black pepper in small bowl. Pour over bean mixture; toss to coat. Cover; refrigerate 2 hours or overnight.

3. Arrange bread slices in single layer on large nonstick baking sheet or broiler pan. Broil, 6 to 8 inches from heat, 30 to 45 seconds or until bread slices are lightly toasted. Remove; cool completely.

4. Top each toasted bread slice with about 3 tablespoons of bean mixture.

Makes 12 servings

TIP Double this recipe and make two appetizers at once. Serve half of the bean mixture on the crostini as directed above. Purée the other half of the mixture in a food processor or blender and serve as a dip with a variety of crisp vegetable dippers.

Tuscan White Bean Crostini

Nutty Carrot Spread

6 ounces fat-free cream cheese, softened
2 tablespoons frozen orange juice concentrate, thawed
¼ teaspoon ground cinnamon
1 cup shredded carrot
¼ cup finely chopped pecans, toasted
¼ cup raisins
36 party pumpernickel bread slices, toasted, or melba toast rounds

1. Combine cream cheese, orange juice concentrate and cinnamon in small bowl; stir until well blended. Stir in carrot, pecans and raisins.

2. Spread about 1 tablespoon cream cheese mixture onto each bread slice.

Makes 18 servings

Cook's Note: To toast pecans, place pecans in shallow baking pan. Bake at 350°F 10 minutes or until lightly toasted, stirring occasionally.

Orange Yogurt Dip for Fresh Fruit

1 carton (8 ounces) low-fat plain yogurt
2 tablespoons honey
Grated peel of ½ SUNKIST® orange
2 SUNKIST® oranges, peeled and segmented
1 medium unpeeled apple, sliced*
1 medium banana, peeled and cut into chunks*

*Sprinkle cut apple and banana with small amount of orange or lemon juice to prevent fruit from darkening.

In small bowl, combine yogurt, honey and orange peel. Serve as dip with oranges, apple and banana.

Makes 4 (2-ounce) servings

Serving Suggestion: To serve in orange shells, cut oranges in half crosswise in middle. Ream juice from both halves. Scrape shells clean with spoon. Cut small slice off bottom of shells so oranges sit flat. Fill as desired. Shells can be made and frozen ahead, to be used at a later date. (Save juice for drinking or use in other recipes.)

Nutty Carrot Spread

Christmas Confetti Dip

1 cup fat-free or reduced-fat sour cream
4 teaspoons dry ranch-style salad dressing mix
¼ cup finely chopped cucumber
¼ cup finely chopped carrot
¼ cup finely chopped red bell pepper
¼ cup finely chopped zucchini

1. Combine sour cream and dressing mix in medium bowl; mix well. Stir in chopped vegetables; cover. Refrigerate 2 to 3 hours for flavors to blend.

2. Transfer dip to medium serving bowl. Garnish with bell pepper cutouts, if desired. Serve with assorted fresh vegetable dippers.

Makes 8 (¼-cup) servings

Dilly of a Dip: Substitute ½ cup finely chopped seeded cucumber for the 1 cup finely chopped vegetables listed above. Stir in 1 to 1½ teaspoons dill weed or dried basil leaves, crushed. Makes about 1¾ cups.

Fresh Veggie Spread: Beat 1½ (8-ounce) packages softened nonfat or reduced-fat cream cheese in medium bowl until creamy. Beat in enough nonfat or reduced-fat sour cream to make desired consistency for spreading. Stir in 3 to 4 tablespoons each chopped red bell pepper, zucchini and carrot. Stir in 1 to 1½ teaspoons dill weed or dried oregano leaves, crushed. Spread onto assorted crackers or party rye bread slices. Makes about 2 cups.

Quick Veggie Spread: Prepare Fresh Veggie Spread, substituting ¼ cup dry vegetable soup mix for the chopped fresh vegetables. Makes about 1½ cups.

Christmas Confetti Dip

Cheesy Potato Skins
with Black Beans & Salsa

6 medium potatoes (6 ounces each), baked
¾ cup GUILTLESS GOURMET® Black Bean Dip (Spicy or Mild)
¾ cup (3 ounces) grated Cheddar cheese
¾ cup GUILTLESS GOURMET® Salsa (Roasted Red Pepper or
Southwestern Grill)
¾ cup low fat sour cream
Fresh cilantro sprigs (optional)

Preheat oven to 400°F. Cut baked potatoes in half lengthwise and scoop out potato pulp, leaving ¼-inch pulp attached to skin (avoid breaking skin). (Save potato pulp for another use, such as mashed potatoes.) Place potato skins on large baking sheet, skin sides down; bake 5 minutes.

Fill each potato skin with 1 tablespoon bean dip and 1 tablespoon cheese. Return to oven; bake 10 minutes. Remove from oven; let cool 5 minutes. Dollop 1 tablespoon salsa and 1 tablespoon sour cream onto each potato. Garnish with cilantro, if desired. Serve hot.   *Makes 12 servings*

Green Pea Mockamole

1 package (16 ounces) frozen petite peas
4 green onions
½ cup lightly packed fresh cilantro
2 tablespoons lemon juice
½ cup GUILTLESS GOURMET® Salsa (Roasted Red Pepper or
Southwestern Grill)
Fresh cilantro sprigs (optional)
1 large bag (7 ounces) GUILTLESS GOURMET® Baked Tortilla
Chips (yellow, red or blue corn)

Cook peas according to package directions; drain. Place peas, onions, ½ cup cilantro and juice in food processor or blender; process until smooth. Transfer to serving bowl; gently stir in salsa to combine. Garnish with cilantro sprigs, if desired. Serve warm with tortilla chips or cover and refrigerate until ready to serve.   *Makes 12 servings*

Cheesy Potato Skins with Black Beans & Salsa

Roasted Eggplant Dip

2 eggplants (about 1 pound each)
¼ cup lemon juice
3 tablespoons sesame tahini*
4 cloves garlic, minced
2 teaspoons hot pepper sauce
½ teaspoon salt
  Paprika
1 tablespoon chopped fresh parsley
  Pita bread rounds, cut into wedges
  Red chili pepper slices (optional)

Available in the ethnic section of the supermarket or in Middle Eastern grocery stores.

Prepare grill for direct cooking. Prick eggplants in several places with fork. Place eggplants on grid. Grill, covered, over medium-high heat 30 to 40 minutes or until skin is black and blistered and pulp is soft, turning often. Peel eggplants when cool enough to handle. Let cool to room temperature.

Place eggplant pulp in food processor with lemon juice, tahini, garlic, pepper sauce and salt; process until smooth. Refrigerate at least 1 hour before serving to allow flavors to blend. Sprinkle top with paprika and parsley; serve with pita bread wedges. Garnish with red chili pepper slices, if desired.

Makes 8 (¼-cup) servings

TIP Tahini is a thick paste made of ground sesame seed and a "must have" for Roasted Eggplant Dip which is also called baba ghanoush. The roasted eggplant imparts a wonderful smoky flavor for a delicious, unique dip.

Roasted Eggplant Dip

Fresh Garden Dip

1½ cups fat-free or reduced-fat mayonnaise
1½ cups shredded DOLE® Carrots
1 cup DOLE® Broccoli, finely chopped
⅓ cup finely chopped green onions
2 teaspoons dried dill weed
¼ teaspoon garlic powder
  DOLE® Cauliflower Florets or Peeled Mini Carrots

• Stir together mayonnaise, shredded carrots, broccoli, green onions, dill and garlic powder in medium bowl until blended.

• Spoon into serving bowl. Cover and chill 1 hour or overnight. Serve with assorted fresh vegetables. Refrigerate any leftovers in airtight container.

Makes 3½ cups

Bruschetta

2 Italian rolls (each 5 inches long)
1 can (14.5 ounces) CONTADINA® Recipe Ready
  Diced Tomatoes, drained
2 tablespoons chopped fresh basil
1 tablespoon finely chopped onion
1 tablespoon olive oil
1 small clove garlic, crushed
¼ teaspoon dried oregano leaves, crushed
¼ teaspoon salt
⅛ teaspoon ground black pepper

1. Slice rolls in half lengthwise; toast.

2. Combine tomatoes, basil, onion, olive oil, garlic, oregano, salt and pepper in small bowl. Spoon mixture onto toasted rolls.

3. Broil 5 inches from heat source, until hot, about 2 minutes.

Makes 8 appetizer servings

Top to bottom: Fresh Garden Dip and
Fiesta Quesadillas with Fruit Salsa (page 194)

187

Herbed-Stuffed Tomatoes

15 **cherry tomatoes**
½ **cup low-fat (1%) cottage cheese**
 1 **tablespoon thinly sliced green onion**
 1 **teaspoon chopped fresh chervil** *or* ¼ **teaspoon dried chervil leaves**
½ **teaspoon snipped fresh dill** *or* ⅛ **teaspoon dried dill weed**
⅛ **teaspoon lemon pepper**

Cut thin slice off bottom of each tomato. Scoop out pulp with small spoon; discard pulp. Invert tomatoes onto paper towels to drain.

Combine cottage cheese, green onion, chervil, dill and lemon pepper in small bowl. Spoon into tomatoes. Serve at once, or cover and refrigerate up to 8 hours. *Makes 5 servings*

Marinated Artichoke Cheese Toasts

 1 **jar (8 ounces) marinated artichoke hearts, drained**
½ **cup (2 ounces) shredded reduced-fat Swiss cheese**
⅓ **cup finely chopped roasted red peppers**
⅓ **cup finely chopped celery**
 1 **tablespoon plus 1½ teaspoons reduced-fat mayonnaise**
24 **melba toast rounds**
   Paprika

1. Rinse artichokes under cold running water; drain well. Pat dry with paper towels. Finely chop artichokes; place in medium bowl. Add cheese, peppers, celery and mayonnaise; mix well.

2. Spoon artichoke mixture evenly onto melba toast rounds; place on large nonstick baking sheet or broiler pan. Broil, 6 inches from heat, about 45 seconds or until cheese mixture is hot and bubbly. Sprinkle with paprika. Garnish, if desired. *Makes 12 servings*

Herbed-Stuffed Tomatoes

Warm Peanut-Caramel Dip

¼ cup reduced-fat peanut butter
2 tablespoons fat-free caramel topping
2 tablespoons fat-free (skim) milk
1 large apple, thinly sliced
4 large pretzel rods, broken in half

1. Combine peanut butter, caramel topping and milk in small saucepan. Heat over low heat, stirring constantly, until mixture is melted and warm.

2. Serve dip with apple and pretzel rods.   *Makes 4 servings*

Microwave Directions: Combine all ingredients except apple and pretzel rods in small microwavable dish. Microwave at MEDIUM (50%) 1 minute; stir well. Microwave an additional minute or until mixture is melted and warm. Serve dip with apple and pretzel rods.

White Bean Dip

1 (16-ounce) can cannellini beans (white kidney beans),
**   rinsed and drained**
1 tablespoon olive oil
2 teaspoons fresh lemon juice
1 clove garlic, sliced
1 teaspoon ground coriander
1 teaspoon TABASCO® brand Pepper Sauce
½ teaspoon ground cumin
¼ teaspoon salt
**   Raw vegetables or pita bread**

Combine all ingredients in food processor except vegetables; process until smooth. Remove to serving bowl and refrigerate until ready to serve. Serve with crisp vegetables such as sliced carrots, celery, cucumber or pita bread triangles.   *Makes 1½ cups*

Warm Peanut-Caramel Dip

Shrimp Dip with Crudités

1 can (6 ounces) cooked shrimp, drained and divided
½ cup reduced-fat cream cheese, softened
⅓ cup plus 1 tablespoon thinly sliced green onions, divided
3 tablespoons light or fat-free Caesar salad dressing
2 teaspoons prepared horseradish
¼ teaspoon salt
2 red or yellow bell peppers, cut into 2×1-inch pieces
4 large carrots, peeled, diagonally sliced ¼-inch thick
10 crispbread or other low-fat crackers

1. Reserve several shrimp for garnish. Combine remaining shrimp, cream cheese, ⅓ cup green onions, salad dressing, horseradish and salt in medium bowl; mix well. Transfer to serving dish; top with reserved shrimp and remaining 1 tablespoon green onions. Cover and chill at least 30 minutes before serving.

2. Serve with bell peppers, carrots and crackers. *Makes 10 servings*

Vegetable Dip

1 cup low fat (1%) cottage cheese
2 tablespoons finely chopped onion
2 tablespoons finely chopped green bell pepper
2 tablespoons finely chopped radish
¼ teaspoon celery salt
Assorted vegetable dippers (optional)

Drain cheese, reserving liquid. Add drained cheese to food processor or blender. (Add 1 to 2 teaspoons of reserved liquid for easier blending.) Process until smooth. Transfer mixture to small bowl; stir in onion, bell pepper, radish and celery salt. Cover; refrigerate at least 1 hour to allow flavors to blend. Serve with vegetable dippers. *Makes 10 servings*

*Favorite recipe from **Wisconsin Milk Marketing Board***

Shrimp Dip with Crudités

Smoked Salmon Appetizers

¼ cup reduced-fat or fat-free cream cheese, softened
1 tablespoon chopped fresh dill *or* 1 teaspoon dried dill weed
⅛ teaspoon ground red pepper
4 ounces thinly sliced smoked salmon or lox
24 melba toast rounds or other low-fat crackers

1. Combine cream cheese, dill and pepper in small bowl; stir to blend. Spread evenly over each slice of salmon. Roll up salmon slices jelly-roll fashion. Place on plate; cover with plastic wrap. Chill at least 1 hour or up to 4 hours before serving.

2. Using sharp knife, cut salmon rolls crosswise into ¾-inch pieces. Place pieces, cut side down, on serving plate. Garnish each salmon roll with dill sprig, if desired. Serve cold or at room temperature with melba rounds.

Makes about 2 dozen appetizers

Fiesta Quesadillas with Fruit Salsa

1 can (11 ounces) DOLE® Mandarin Oranges, drained and finely chopped
1 tablespoon chopped fresh cilantro or fresh parsley
1 tablespoon lime juice
4 (8-inch) whole wheat or flour tortillas
¾ cup shredded low fat Monterey Jack, mozzarella or Cheddar cheese
⅔ cup finely chopped DOLE® Pitted Dates or Chopped Dates or finely chopped Pitted Prunes
⅓ cup crumbled feta cheese
2 tablespoons chopped green onion

• Combine mandarin oranges, cilantro and lime juice in small bowl for salsa; set aside.

• Place two tortillas on large baking sheet. Sprinkle half of shredded cheese, dates, feta and green onion over each tortilla to within ½ inch of edge.

continued on page 196

Smoked Salmon Appetizers

- Brush outer ½-inch edge of each tortilla with water. Top with remaining tortillas; press down edges gently to seal.

- Bake at 375°F 5 to 8 minutes or until hot. Cut each quesadilla into 6 wedges.

- Drain salsa just before serving, if desired; serve over warm quesadillas.

Makes 6 servings

Prep Time: 15 minutes
Bake Time: 8 minutes

Fresh Tomato Eggplant Spread

1 medium eggplant
2 large ripe tomatoes, seeded and chopped
1 cup minced zucchini
¼ cup chopped green onions with tops
2 tablespoons red wine vinegar
1 tablespoon olive oil
1 teaspoon honey
1 clove garlic, minced
1 tablespoon minced fresh basil
2 teaspoons minced fresh oregano
1 teaspoon minced fresh thyme
⅛ teaspoon black pepper
¼ cup pine nuts or slivered almonds
32 melba toast rounds

1. Preheat oven to 375°F. Poke holes in surface of eggplant with fork. Bake 20 to 25 minutes or until tender. Cool completely; peel and mince. Place in colander; press to release excess water.

2. Combine eggplant with tomatoes, zucchini, green onions, vinegar, oil, honey, garlic, basil, oregano, thyme and black pepper in large bowl. Mix well. Refrigerate 2 hours to allow flavors to blend.

3. Stir in pine nuts just before serving. Serve with melba toast rounds.

Makes 8 servings

Fresh Tomato Eggplant Spread

CRUNCHY SNACKS

Nicole's Cheddar Crisps

1¾ **cups all-purpose flour**
½ **cup yellow cornmeal**
¾ **teaspoon sugar**
¾ **teaspoon salt**
½ **teaspoon baking soda**
½ **cup (1 stick) butter or margarine**
1½ **cups (6 ounces) shredded sharp Cheddar cheese**
½ **cup cold water**
2 **tablespoons white vinegar**
Coarsely ground black pepper

Mix flour, cornmeal, sugar, salt and baking soda in large bowl. Cut in butter with pastry blender until mixture resembles coarse crumbs. Stir in cheese, water and vinegar with fork until mixture forms soft dough. Cover dough and refrigerate 1 hour or freeze 30 minutes until firm.

Preheat oven to 375°F. Grease 2 large cookie sheets. Divide dough into 4 pieces. Roll each piece into paper-thin circle (about 13 inches in diameter) on floured surface. Sprinkle with pepper; press pepper firmly into dough.

Cut each circle into 8 wedges; place wedges on prepared cookie sheets. Bake about 10 minutes or until crisp. Store in airtight container for up to 3 days. *Makes 32 crisps*

Nicole's Cheddar Crisps

Parmesan Ranch Snack Mix

- 3 **cups bite-size corn or rice cereal**
- 2 **cups oyster crackers**
- 1 **package (5 ounces) bagel chips, broken in half**
- 1½ **cups pretzel twists**
- 1 **cup pistachios**
- 2 **tablespoons grated Parmesan cheese**
- ¼ **cup butter, melted**
- 1 **package (1 ounce) dry ranch salad dressing mix**
- ½ **teaspoon garlic powder**

SLOW COOKER DIRECTIONS

1. Combine cereal, oyster crackers, bagel chips, pretzels, pistachios and Parmesan cheese in slow cooker; mix gently.

2. Combine butter, salad dressing mix and garlic powder in small bowl. Pour over cereal mixture; toss lightly to coat. Cover; cook on LOW 3 hours. Remove cover and stir gently. Continue to cook, uncovered, on LOW 30 minutes. *Makes about 9½ cups snack mix*

Deviled Mixed Nuts

- 3 **tablespoons vegetable oil**
- 2 **cups assorted unsalted nuts, such as peanuts, almonds, Brazil nuts or walnuts**
- 2 **tablespoons sugar**
- 1 **teaspoon paprika**
- ½ **teaspoon chili powder**
- ½ **teaspoon curry powder**
- ½ **teaspoon ground cumin**
- ½ **teaspoon ground coriander**
- ½ **teaspoon black pepper**
- ¼ **teaspoon salt**

Heat oil in large skillet over medium heat; cook and stir nuts in hot oil 2 to 3 minutes or until browned. Combine remaining ingredients in small bowl; sprinkle over nuts. Stir to coat evenly. Heat 1 to 2 minutes more. Drain nuts on wire rack lined with paper towels. Serve warm. *Makes 2 cups*

Parmesan Ranch Snack Mix

Party Mix

3 cups bite-size rice cereal
2 cups O-shaped oat cereal
2 cups bite-size shredded wheat cereal
1 cup peanuts or pistachios
1 cup thin pretzel sticks
½ cup butter, melted
1 tablespoon Worcestershire sauce
1 teaspoon seasoned salt
½ teaspoon garlic powder
⅛ teaspoon ground red pepper (optional)

SLOW COOKER DIRECTIONS

1. Combine cereals, nuts and pretzels in slow cooker.

2. Mix melted butter, Worcestershire sauce, seasoned salt, garlic powder and red pepper in small bowl. Pour over cereal mixture in slow cooker; toss lightly to coat.

3. Cover; cook on LOW 3 hours, stirring well every 30 minutes. Remove cover; cook an additional 30 minutes. Store in airtight container.

Makes 10 cups

TIP **Serve this make-ahead recipe in an assortment of colorful small bowls such as wooden salad bowls, colorful cereal bowls or even a variety of plastic storage containers. Then, place the bowls throughout the party area for easy access by all the guests.**

Party Mix

Bacon-Wrapped Breadsticks

8 slices bacon
16 garlic-flavored breadsticks (about 8 inches long)
¾ cup grated Parmesan cheese
2 tablespoons chopped fresh parsley (optional)

Cut bacon slices in half lengthwise. Wrap half slice of bacon diagonally around each breadstick. Combine Parmesan cheese and parsley, if desired, in shallow dish; set aside.

Place 4 breadsticks on double layer of paper towels in microwave oven. Microwave on HIGH 2 to 3 minutes or until bacon is cooked through. Immediately roll breadsticks in Parmesan mixture to coat. Repeat with remaining breadsticks. *Makes 16 breadsticks*

Cajun-Spiced Walnuts

1 egg white, slightly beaten
1½ tablespoons garlic salt
1½ teaspoons mixed dried herbs
1 teaspoon ground cayenne pepper
1 teaspoon paprika
2 cups (1 pound) California walnut halves and pieces

Preheat oven to 350°F. Coat large, shallow baking pan with nonstick vegetable spray. Mix in large bowl the egg white, garlic salt, herbs, cayenne and paprika. Stir in walnuts and coat thoroughly. Spread in prepared baking pan. Bake in 350°F oven 15 to 18 minutes, stirring once after 8 minutes, until dry and crisp. Cool completely before serving. Store in airtight container.

Makes 2 cups

Microwave Directions: Prepare ingredients as above. Spread prepared walnuts in microwavable dish. Microwave on HIGH in 4 or 5 batches for 2 to 3 minutes each, until dry and crisp. Cool completely.

Note: Best if made at least one day ahead. Flavors intensify overnight. Store in sealed container.

*Favorite recipe from **Walnut Marketing Board***

Bacon-Wrapped Breadsticks

Cheese Twists

1 cup all-purpose flour
½ teaspoon baking soda
½ teaspoon salt
½ teaspoon dry mustard
⅛ teaspoon ground red pepper
¾ cup grated Parmesan cheese, divided
½ cup butter or margarine, softened
3 egg yolks
2 teaspoons water
1 egg white, lightly beaten
1 tablespoon sesame seeds (optional)

Preheat oven to 400°F. Grease two cookie sheets. Combine flour, baking soda, salt, mustard and red pepper in large bowl. Reserve 1 tablespoon cheese; stir remaining cheese into flour mixture. Cut in butter with pastry blender or 2 knives until mixture resembles fine crumbs. Add egg yolks and water, mixing until dough forms. Shape into a ball; flatten and wrap in plastic wrap. Refrigerate 2 hours or until firm.

Roll out dough on lightly floured surface into 12-inch square (about ⅛ inch thick). Brush surface lightly with egg white and sprinkle with remaining 1 tablespoon cheese and sesame seeds, if desired. Cut dough in half. Cut each half crosswise into ¼-inch strips. Twist 2 strips together. Repeat with remaining strips. Place 1 inch apart on prepared cookie sheets.

Bake 6 to 8 minutes or until light golden brown. Remove from cookie sheets and cool completely on wire racks. Store in airtight container.

Makes about 48 twists

Variation: Prepare dough and cut as directed. Place ¾ of strips on cookie sheets. Form rings with remaining strips; seal edges. Place on cookie sheets. Bake and cool as directed. To serve, arrange 3 to 4 strips into small stacks. Insert stacks into rings.

CRUNCHY SNACKS

From left to right: Cheese Twists and
Deviled Mixed Nuts (page 200)

Spiced Sesame Wonton Crisps

20 (3-inch-square) wonton wrappers, cut in half
1 tablespoon water
2 teaspoons olive oil
½ teaspoon paprika
½ teaspoon ground cumin or chili powder
¼ teaspoon dry mustard
1 tablespoon sesame seeds

1. Preheat oven to 375°F. Coat 2 large nonstick baking sheets with nonstick cooking spray.

2. Cut each halved wonton wrapper into 2 strips; place in single layer on prepared baking sheets.

3. Combine water, oil, paprika, cumin and mustard in small bowl; mix well. Brush oil mixture evenly onto wonton strips; sprinkle evenly with sesame seeds.

4. Bake 6 to 8 minutes or until lightly browned. Remove to wire rack; cool completely. Transfer to serving plate.   *Makes 8 servings*

"M&M's"® Family Party Mix

2 tablespoons butter or margarine*
¼ cup honey*
2 cups favorite grain cereal or 3 cups granola
1 cup coarsely chopped nuts
1 cup thin pretzel pieces
1 cup raisins
2 cups "M&M's"® Chocolate Mini Baking Bits

*For a drier mix, eliminate butter and honey. Simply combine dry ingredients and do not bake.

Preheat oven to 300°F. In large saucepan over low heat, melt butter; add honey until well blended. Remove from heat and add cereal, nuts, pretzel pieces and raisins, stirring until all pieces are evenly coated. Spread mixture onto ungreased cookie sheet and bake about 10 minutes. Do not overbake. Spread mixture onto waxed paper and allow to cool completely. In large bowl combine mixture and "M&M's"® Chocolate Mini Baking Bits. Store in tightly covered container.   *Makes about 6 cups snack mix*

Spiced Sesame Wonton Crisps

Honey Popcorn Clusters

Vegetable cooking spray
6 cups air-popped popcorn
⅔ cup DOLE® Golden or Seedless Raisins
½ cup DOLE® Chopped Dates or Pitted Dates, chopped
⅓ cup almonds (optional)
⅓ cup packed brown sugar
¼ cup honey
2 tablespoons margarine
¼ teaspoon baking soda

• Line bottom and sides of 13×9-inch baking pan with large sheet of aluminum foil. Spray foil with vegetable cooking spray.

• Stir together popcorn, raisins, dates and almonds in foil-lined pan.

• Combine brown sugar, honey and margarine in small saucepan. Bring to boil over medium heat, stirring constantly; reduce heat to low. Cook 5 minutes. *Do not stir.* Remove from heat.

• Stir in baking soda. Pour evenly over popcorn mixture, stirring quickly to coat mixture evenly.

• Bake at 300°F 12 to 15 minutes or until mixture is lightly browned, stirring once halfway through baking time.

• Lift foil from pan; place on cooling rack. Cool popcorn mixture completely; break into clusters. Popcorn can be stored in airtight container up to 1 week.

Makes 7 cups

Prep Time: 20 minutes
Bake Time: 15 minutes

Honey Popcorn Clusters

Cheesy Sun Crisps

- **2 cups (8 ounces) shredded Cheddar cheese**
- **½ cup grated Parmesan cheese**
- **½ cup sunflower oil margarine, softened**
- **3 tablespoons water**
- **1 cup all-purpose flour**
- **¼ teaspoon salt (optional)**
- **1 cup uncooked quick oats**
- **⅔ cup roasted, salted sunflower seeds**

Beat cheeses, margarine and water in bowl until blended. Mix in flour and salt. Stir in oats and sunflower seeds until combined. Shape into 12-inch-long roll; wrap securely. Refrigerate about 4 hours or up to 1 week.

Preheat oven to 400°F. Lightly grease cookie sheets. Cut roll into ⅛- to ¼-inch slices; flatten each slice slightly. Place on prepared cookie sheets. Bake 8 to 10 minutes or until edges are light golden brown. Remove immediately; cool on wire rack. *Makes 4 to 5 dozen crackers*

*Favorite recipe from **National Sunflower Association***

Hot 'n' Spicy Italian Stix Mix

- **6 tablespoons butter or margarine, melted**
- **2 tablespoons *Frank's® RedHot®* Cayenne Pepper Sauce**
- **1 tablespoon *French's®* Worcestershire Sauce**
- **4 cups oven-toasted rice cereal squares**
- **2⅔ cups *French's®* French Fried Onions, divided**
- **2 cans (1½ ounces each) *French's®* Potato Sticks**
- **¼ cup grated Parmesan cheese**
- **1 package (1.25 ounces) Italian spaghetti sauce mix**

1. Preheat oven to 250°F. Combine butter, *Frank's RedHot* Sauce and Worcestershire in glass measuring cup. Place remaining ingredients in shallow roasting pan; mix well. Pour butter mixture over cereal mixture; toss to coat evenly.

2. Bake 30 minutes or until crispy, stirring twice. Cool completely.

Makes 7 cups mix

Praline Pecans & Cranberries

Sun-Dried Tomato Pizza Snack Mix

2 cups wheat cereal squares
2 cups unsweetened puffed corn cereal
2 cups crisp rice cereal
2 cups square mini cheese crackers
1 cup roasted sunflower seeds
3 tablespoons grated Parmesan cheese
3 tablespoons butter
2 tablespoons olive oil
2 teaspoons dried Italian seasoning
1½ teaspoons garlic powder
¼ cup tomato sauce
1 teaspoon balsamic vinegar
¼ teaspoon sugar
⅛ teaspoon salt
8 to 9 sun-dried tomatoes packed in oil, diced

1. Preheat oven to 250°F. Spray 13×9-inch baking pan with nonstick cooking spray.

2. Combine cereals, cheese crackers and sunflower seeds in large bowl; set aside.

3. Combine cheese, butter, oil, Italian seasoning and garlic powder in medium bowl. Microwave at HIGH 1 to 1½ minutes until foamy and herbs release their aromas. Stir in tomato sauce, vinegar, sugar and salt. Pour over cereal mixture; stir well to coat. Place in prepared pan and spread in single layer.

4. Bake 55 to 60 minutes, stirring every 15 minutes. Stir in sun-dried tomatoes 15 minutes before finished baking. Cool in pan on wire rack about 2 hours, leaving uncovered until mixture is crisp and tomato pieces have lost their moisture. Store in airtight container or resealable plastic food storage bag. *Makes 7 cups*

Sun-Dried Tomato Pizza Snack Mix

The publisher would like to thank the companies and organizations listed below for the use of their recipes and photographs in this publication.

BC-USA, Inc.
BelGioioso® Cheese, Inc.
Birds Eye®
Bob Evans®
Butterball® Turkey Company
Cherry Marketing Institute
Del Monte Corporation
Dole Food Company, Inc.
Filippo Berio® Olive Oil
The Golden Grain Company®
Guiltless Gourmet®
Heinz North America
The Hidden Valley® Food Products Company
Hillshire Farm®
© Mars, Incorporated 2003
McIlhenny Company (TABASCO® brand Pepper Sauce)
Mushroom Council
National Onion Association
National Pork Board
National Sunflower Association
National Turkey Federation
Norseland, Inc. / Lucini Italia Co.
North Dakota Beef Commission
Ortega®
Peanut Advisory Board
Reckitt Benckiser Inc.
Sargento® Foods Inc.
The J.M. Smucker Company
Sonoma® Dried Tomatoes
Southeast United Dairy Industry Association, Inc.
StarKist® Seafood Company
The Sugar Association, Inc.
Property of © 2003 Sunkist Growers, Inc. All rights reserved.
Unilever Bestfoods North America
USA Rice Federation
Walnut Marketing Board
Wisconsin Milk Marketing Board

A

Alouette® Elégante with Red Pepper Coulis, 26
Antipasto Crescent Bites, 138
Artichoke Frittata, 10
Artichoke Hearts
Antipasto Crescent Bites, 138
Artichoke Frittata, 10
Awesome Antipasto, 22
Cold Artichoke Dip, 6
Creamy Artichoke-Parmesan Dip, 52
Herbed Garlic & Artichoke Dip, 62
Hot Artichoke Dip, 6, 58
Marinated Artichoke Cheese Toasts, 188
Ranch Artichoke Dip, 32
Roasted Red Pepper and Artichoke Torte, 84
Spinach-Artichoke Party Cups, 114
Arugula-Prosciutto Wrapped Breadsticks with Garlic Mustard Sauce, 161
Awesome Antipasto, 22

B

Bacon
Bacon-Wrapped Breadsticks, 204
BLT Dip, 58
Elegant Pork Terrine, 162
Festive Bacon & Cheese Dip, 54
Nutty Bacon Cheeseball, 18
Ranch Bacon Cheddar Dip, 54
Sausage-Bacon-Apricot Kabobs, 120
Barbecue Pizza, 92
Beans
Chavrie® Quesadilla, 42
Cheesy Potato Skins with Black Beans & Salsa, 182
Hummus Vegetable Dip, 69
Mini ChickPea Cakes, 112
Ortega® 7-Layer Dip, 8
Prize-Winning Party-Size Bean Dip, 77
Tortilla Pizzettes, 82

Beans *(continued)*
Tuscan White Bean Crostini, 176
Vegetable Hummus, 52
White Bean Dip, 190
Beef, Ground
Glazed Meatballs, 110
Nacho Bacho, 82
Pizza Snack Cups, 30
Swedish-Style Meatballs, 100
Sweet and Sour Meatballs, 13
BelGioioso Gorgonzola Spread, 40
BLT Dip, 58
Brandied Apricot Brie, 30
Bread & Roll Dough
Antipasto Crescent Bites, 138
Chicken Pesto Pizza, 102
Dried Tomato Party Pockets, 132
Festive Franks, 24
Herb Cheese Twists, 36
Onion and Pepper Calzones, 124
Piggy Wraps, 28
Pizza Snack Cups, 30
Breads
Arugula-Prosciutto Wrapped Breadsticks with Garlic Mustard Sauce, 161
Cheese Straws, 20
Cheese Twists, 206
Crispy Parmesan Pita Chips, 214
Garlic Toasts, 174
Herb Cheese Twists, 36
Brie
Brandied Apricot Brie, 30
Brie Torte, 156
Crème de Brie Phyllo Tartlets with Caramelized Onion, 160
Piña Colada Brie, 170
Broccoli
Fresh Garden Dip, 186
Hot Broccoli Dip, 76
Nutty Broccoli Spread, 66
Savory Peanut Butter Dip, 70
Tortellini Kabobs, 136

Bruschetta, 186
Buffalo-Style Chicken Nachos, 24

C

Cajun-Spiced Walnuts, 204
Celebration Cheese Ball, 74
Chavrie® Quesadilla, 42
Cheddar Chili Tomato Pots, 130
Cheese & Sausage Bundles, 106
Cheese Chili Dip, 64
Cheese Straws, 20
Cheese Twists, 206
Cheesy Mustard Dip, 72
Cheesy Potato Skins with Black Beans & Salsa, 182
Cheesy Snack Squares, 98
Cheesy Sun Crisps, 212
Chicken
Barbecue Pizza, 92
Buffalo-Style Chicken Nachos, 24
Chicken Empanadas, 118
Chicken Nachos, 34
Chicken Pesto Pizza, 102
Chicken-Rice Roll Ups, 97
Golden Chicken Nuggets, 44
Ranch Chicken Tenders, 49
Thai Satay Chicken Skewers, 126
Walnut Chicken Pinwheels, 92
Zesty Liver Pâté, 6
Chicken Wings
Gorgonzola Buffalo Wings, 12
Honey-Mustard Chicken Wings, 80
Jerk Wings with Ranch Dipping Sauce, 88
Original Ranch® Drummettes, 102
Chicken Empanadas, 118
Chicken Nachos, 34
Chicken Pesto Pizza, 102
Chicken-Rice Roll Ups, 97
Chili Dip, 64
Christmas Confetti Dip, 180
Chutney Cheese Spread, 62
Cocktail Bites, 32

METRIC CONVERSION CHART

VOLUME MEASUREMENTS (dry)

1/8 teaspoon = 0.5 mL
1/4 teaspoon = 1 mL
1/2 teaspoon = 2 mL
3/4 teaspoon = 4 mL
1 teaspoon = 5 mL
1 tablespoon = 15 mL
2 tablespoons = 30 mL
1/4 cup = 60 mL
1/3 cup = 75 mL
1/2 cup = 125 mL
2/3 cup = 150 mL
3/4 cup = 175 mL
1 cup = 250 mL
2 cups = 1 pint = 500 mL
3 cups = 750 mL
4 cups = 1 quart = 1 L

VOLUME MEASUREMENTS (fluid)

1 fluid ounce (2 tablespoons) = 30 mL
4 fluid ounces (1/2 cup) = 125 mL
8 fluid ounces (1 cup) = 250 mL
12 fluid ounces (1 1/2 cups) = 375 mL
16 fluid ounces (2 cups) = 500 mL

WEIGHTS (mass)

1/2 ounce = 15 g
1 ounce = 30 g
3 ounces = 90 g
4 ounces = 120 g
8 ounces = 225 g
10 ounces = 285 g
12 ounces = 360 g
16 ounces = 1 pound = 450 g

DIMENSIONS

1/16 inch = 2 mm
1/8 inch = 3 mm
1/4 inch = 6 mm
1/2 inch = 1.5 cm
3/4 inch = 2 cm
1 inch = 2.5 cm

OVEN TEMPERATURES

250°F = 120°C
275°F = 140°C
300°F = 150°C
325°F = 160°C
350°F = 180°C
375°F = 190°C
400°F = 200°C
425°F = 220°C
450°F = 230°C

BAKING PAN SIZES

Utensil	Size in Inches/Quarts	Metric Volume	Size in Centimeters
Baking or Cake Pan (square or rectangular)	8×8×2	2 L	20×20×5
	9×9×2	2.5 L	23×23×5
	12×8×2	3 L	30×20×5
	13×9×2	3.5 L	33×23×5
Loaf Pan	8×4×3	1.5 L	20×10×7
	9×5×3	2 L	23×13×7
Round Layer Cake Pan	8×1½	1.2 L	20×4
	9×1½	1.5 L	23×4
Pie Plate	8×1¼	750 mL	20×3
	9×1¼	1 L	23×3
Baking Dish or Casserole	1 quart	1 L	—
	1½ quart	1.5 L	—
	2 quart	2 L	—